Praying With God

Releasing Heaven on Earth through the Power of the Lord's Prayer

By Pastor Darren Farmer

ISBN 9781791899448

Imprint: Independently Published

Acknowledgements

To my beautiful wife, Amanda. Thank you for going on another God adventure with me. Thank you for your patience during the many hours alone as I typed away on another book and for the words of encouragement when I didn't want to write anymore. Thank you for always believing in me. You are truly my inspiration.

To Dena Boucher for the countless hours of reading and editing. You have embraced this project with great joy and enthusiasm which is contagious and refreshing.

Dedication

I want to dedicate this book to my wonderful children; Katelynn, Brooklynn, Connor, and Addalynn. As I write about the love of our heavenly Father, I am inspired to become a better dad. I pray that as you read this book, you will see a reflection of His heart in mine. I love you!

CONTENTS

Introduction - The Lord's Prayer

One of the twelve disciples asked Jesus a great question which was met with a direct answer. This, in itself, is unusual as Jesus often answered a question with a riddle, a parable, or an answer wrapped in mystery. The question he asked is one that many of us have asked. "Lord, will you teach us to pray?" I do not believe he was asking for a way to be more spiritual, but he was asking how to get answers to his prayers.

The disciple was looking for supernatural breakthrough. He probably thought his answer could be found in a formula. Perhaps his real question was, "What do I need to do to get what I need to have?" This was a typical, culturally Jewish way of thinking at that time. Like many Jews, he would have been brought up in a culture that had an understanding of a covenant keeping God.

This is how it worked in accordance with the old covenant as seen in the Old Testament. When God made a covenant with man, it required an agreement. If you did this, if you kept the law or kept your part of the bargain, then God would bless you. If you do what you want to do and it is in opposition to the agreement you have made with God, you will be breaking the law. By doing so, you have chosen to walk in disobedience. Because you broke the law you will no longer receive blessings, but curses.

The covenant agreement was based on two parties keeping their part of the deal and therefore experiencing the reward of the covenant or the agreement that they had made together. This thinking would have influenced the disciple asking the question. In other words, he was asking Jesus what he needed to do so he would find favor and experience the blessings of God.

I am sure that when this disciple approached Jesus he knew that God was able to bless, move miraculously, and do the impossible. He had heard the stories of past answers to prayer and he had seen Jesus in action. The questions on his heart were "How do I access the blessings of God? How do I pray in a way that will bring answers? What do I need to do to ensure that God hears me and answers me?" As I said at the beginning, this man asked a question in the presence of the other disciples. It's a question that they and we want answered. We want to know how to get our prayers answered!

At a glance, it looks like Jesus answered him in a way he would understand with a list of things to do or with a formula in which to pray. But as we look closer, we see that Jesus was inviting him into a relationship with the Father. He was teaching him how to pray *with* God and not just *to* God. He wanted him and everyone who prays the Lord's Prayer to experience more than just the breakthrough or miracle. He wanted them to know the one who brings the breakthrough.

Like many of you, I have prayed this prayer in school and church many times. I have taken it further and broken each section down and used each part as a point of prayer. In these ways, I have gained insight, hope, and have seen prayers answered. As I have developed my prayer life and continued to study this scripture in the light of the New Testament, I have gained a greater revelation and truth. The basis of us receiving from God is not interwoven in an old covenant as seen through the pages of the Old Testament. Our answers lie in a new covenant; a better covenant with even better promises.

① For what credit is it if, when you sin & are beaten for it, you endure? But if when you do good & suffer for it you endure, this is a gracious thing in the sight of God.

The terms and conditions of this new covenant are so much better and make it much easier for prayers to be answered. It is more than a list of things we should do or pray for God to hear our request. It's more than us trying to twist His arm and convince Him to move on our behalf.

The old covenant proved that man could not live up to the demands or the rules of the agreement. As we look throughout the Old Testament, we see man failing and falling short at every turn.

Once it was made clear that man could not live up to the demands of the covenant, the Father revealed His master plan. It was a plan that had been hidden in the Father's heart before the creation of the world. (1 Peter 2:20) ①

How would the Father release the blessings and promises of a covenant and answer the prayers of our hearts when man could not live up to the agreement of the covenant or contract? This was a mystery!

Hidden within all of the sacrifices of the old covenant is a story. It is a story written with types and shadows in the very fabric and vessels of the tabernacle. There were revelations declared throughout the many prophetic words that had been spoken over Israel. It was a master plan discovered in His only begotten son, Jesus.

The only way to release the blessings of God and therefore answer our prayer without obstruction was by making the covenant with Jesus, and not with man.

Jesus was the perfect solution! He was known as "the lamb without blemish." He who knew no sin would become our sacrifice for sin. He would offer His own blood with whom He would "cut covenant" or make a covenant with the Father. His offering was accepted and

① this makes Jesus the guarantor of a better covenant.

now, Jesus stands as the surety of the covenant at the right hand of the Father, interceding on our behalf. (Hebrews 7:22)①

Our access in relationship to the Father is not because we are good or because we always make the right choices. It's because we have been made righteous through Christ. When we accepted Him as Lord and Savior, we gained access to the promises and blessings of the covenant through Christ.

> For _all_ the promises of God in Him are Yes, and in Him Amen, to the glory of God through us. (2 Corinthians 1:20)

Let's take notice that through Christ, all the promises have been released and there is no mention of curses. That is because Jesus came and took the curse for us on the cross. The curses have been broken and removed. We have been left with blessings!

Go back and read all of the promises connected with every covenant that has been made throughout the Bible. Read every promise of healing, deliverance, provision, and so much more. All of these promises are yours in Christ. Paul tells us that heaven is loaded with every spiritual blessing. (Ephesians 1:3)

This should give us great confidence in prayer. The writer of the book of Hebrews, who is armed with this great revelation, declares that we should come boldly into His presence. (Hebrews 10:19)

We are not coming to a God who makes it difficult for us to approach Him. He has taken every barrier away through the sacrifice of His Son so we can come into His presence. This is a place that has no closed doors or time restraints. He is always available to us.

Jesus, in describing the Lord's Prayer, was not giving the disciples or us a list of things that we must do to get the answers we need. He was giving us direct access to the Father. He was calling us into a relationship with God. This is an invitation to come to God as our Father and to understand His heart and nature.

As we express the longing of our hearts through prayer, we grasp the desire and passion that the Father has for the same things. The added bonus is that every barrier that may have restricted the blessings of heaven being released to us because of our failings have been taken away by Christ's obedience.

Once we come boldly before the Father in prayer and understand how He sees a need, it often changes the way we perceive our needs. We stop seeing them as a problem and begin viewing them as a possibility for heaven to move on earth. Our challenges are an invitation to call out to God and see Him move and reveal His glory.

It is in this relationship with the Father that we start to catch a glimpse of the answer. As our vision changes, faith arises in our hearts and that which seemed impossible now seems possible. The walls of fear or hopelessness come crashing down. Trust is established as our relationship with the Father is developed.

The Lord's Prayer is an invitation into relationship with the Father at a higher level. It is through our relationship with the Father that answers to our prayers are guaranteed.

As we continue our journey through this book with the Lord's Prayer, I desire to reveal to you a different way of thinking. I want you to see the incredible position God has given us to pray with Him and not just to Him.

I do not approach this subject lightly as I know there are many ways to pray and in this book we are dealing with the "holy grail" of prayer. There are many approaches to prayer depending on our circumstance, the needs we have, and the season we are living in.

Prayer can be in the form of intercession, supplication, spiritual warfare, and at times, being still. There are times of individual prayer and corporate prayer. There are occasions in which we call for the elders. We may call a friend to stand with us as we wrestle with needs, for faith, and for a particular outcome.

As we understand the Lord's Prayer, we will better understand relationship and the nature of God which should have an impact in every area of prayer.

This book is my offering on the Lord's Prayer which I have understood through my relationship with God. The Father's invitation for us to pray is so much more than us making requests to Him. It is an invitation to understand His heart and nature and to pray *with* Him! It is about asking for the things He desires to see, declaring the things He reveals to us, and calling into existence the very things that have been hidden in His heart for such a time as this.

Join me in this adventure with our heavenly Father as we take prayer out of the closet of confusion and we come to His table of fellowship. This is the place where relationship is developed, discussions take place, mysteries are revealed, request are made, and prayers are answered.

Luke 11:1-4

Now it came to pass, as He was praying in a certain place, when He ceased, that one of His disciples said to Him, "Lord, teach us to pray, as John also taught his disciples." So He said to them,

"When you pray, say:"

Our Father in heaven,
Hallowed be Your name.
Your kingdom come.
Your will be done
On earth as it is in heaven.
Give us day by day our daily bread.
And forgive us our sins,
For we also forgive everyone who is indebted to us.
And do not lead us into temptation,
But deliver us from the evil one.

Matthew 6:13b adds the following verse:

For Yours is the kingdom and the power and the glory forever.
Amen.

Chapter 1: Our Father

In this manner, therefore, pray: <u>Our Father in heaven</u>, Hallowed be your name. (Matthew 6:9)

Praying with God – Our Father

Many people find prayer to be difficult. They wait until they come to a place in which they have no other solution to the challenges they face. Their only option is to pray. They hope that the God of the universe will hear their cry and answer their prayers.

In calling out to God this way, they already have a misguided image in their mind. They picture Him as the creator God and not "Our Father" God. They see Him to be distant and untouchable; one who cannot relate to the things they are going through. Still, they hope He will hear their prayer and come near and meet their needs.

They have been told that God is looking to punish and judge all that is wrong. They see Him as someone who holds a stick in His hand. They wonder if this God who has been depicted as an angry God would be concerned with their small needs. After all, He has the universe to keep together.

Or maybe they have a view that other people's needs are more important than theirs. As their need grows and the solutions seem to be out of sight, they have no other option but to pray. They call out to an unknown God with a question of doubt in their minds. "Will God hear me or even care about my problem?"

Unfortunately, the God they are looking to and hoping will grant mercy will not answer their prayers. It's not that they are not important to Him or that their prayers are irrelevant. It's that they have a wrong picture of who He is.

The God that longs to answer their prayers and ours is not far off and untouchable. He is very real and personable. He cares about the things we care about. In fact, the things we care about often start in the heart of God. We have caught a part of our Father's heart. Our desires can often be a reflection of our Father's desires.

Jesus introduces the only true God to us in the Lord's Prayer as the Father, a Father, or to quote the scripture "Our Father!" Wow, this amazes me. He doesn't want you to know Him as someone else's Father, but *your* Father.

Many of you have come from broken homes or families with absent fathers. Maybe you have visited the homes of your friends and have seen the kindness of their father and experienced his kindness to you. This, in itself, is refreshing. For many, this is also true of God the Father. You have heard about Him or perhaps have seen how He has moved in other people's lives. They have talked about the comfort and the many things they have experienced through His love. Now it is your turn. God the Father, who you have seen being good and kind to others, wants to show you the same kindness. He wants to invite you into His family and become your Father; a Father you can approach at any time.

This is seen in the life of Jesus who declared "If you have seen me you have seen my Father." In other words, the nature of God in Jesus is a direct reflection of the nature of the Father. So what Jesus does is also what the Father in heaven does. Jesus said "I only do what I see my Father do; for whatever He does, the Son also does in like manner." (John 5:19)

Jesus demonstrated the Father's great love toward children. This really confused the disciples because they had no framework to understand this kind of fatherly love. (Mark 10:13-16) Jesus, like "Our Father" does not keep us, His children, at arm's length. He is not offended by our childish playful desire to run into His waiting arms. With great joy and with a smile on His face, He welcomes us.

Without a care or fear of rejection, the children came to Jesus and He received them gladly. He held them and blessed them. Jesus rejects the stoic, religious position of the disciples and the religious world who are shocked by His willing acceptance of the children. He rebuked the disciples for having a wrong world view of how they thought He should receive them. Not only did the disciples have to go through a paradigm shift in their thinking, so do we as His children. He is waiting for us to run into His arms.

We need to understand the heart of the Father who loves for us to come to Him as children. Jesus corrected the thinking of the disciples by creating a new idea. Jesus said, "Whoever does not receive the kingdom of God as a little child will by no means enter it." (Mark 10:15) Little child meaning small child or infant.

Infants do not have boundaries or rules on how they should approach parents, Jesus, or the Father. In fact, infants will interrupt what you are doing and come as they are at any time. They come with confidence believing that you will notice them and give them attention.

The way we see Jesus or the Father is very important. Children are good at discerning or reading the body language of adults. I believe that when the children saw Jesus, they saw someone who was happy to see them. He was inviting in the way He reached out to them. Perhaps He communicated with a smile or with eyes that were alive with joy and acceptance.

If a parent seems inviting and happy to see their children, the children will respond in kind. We have all seen the cute smile of a baby responding to their parents or the joy of a child when their mother or father returns home from work.

We have also seen fear if a child feels like they are in danger or are not accepted. If we have a view of God as a tyrant father, then we will avoid him at all costs. If we see the love of the Father, we will run toward Him as often as we can. We will not wonder about our acceptance and therefore, our requests or prayers become easier to bring.

Jesus set a new standard and way of thinking when He invited the children to come. The children had as much value in the kingdom as the disciples did. I love this because Jesus not only gives permission to come to Him, He shows His pleasure by blessing them.

Oh, how the Father loves for you to come boldly as little children before Him. (Hebrew 10:19) The invitation is to come as often as you desire, to sit with Him, talk with Him, and receive all the gifts and blessings that come from Him. (Ephesians 1:3)

It is just like the father in the story of the prodigal son. God is not only waiting, but He is watching for us to come to Him. As soon as we make a move toward Him, He runs with open arms toward us. His intention is to lavish us with affection and love. He is ready to listen to your requests. He has been waiting for this moment and His answer will blow you away and far exceed your expectation. (Ephesians 3:20)

The invitation to prayer is an invitation into relationship between the Father and His sons and daughters. That's you! He longs for you to cultivate this relationship by knowing His heart and nature in response to the needs and cares you bring in prayer.

Perhaps it would be helpful to create a better picture of what we call prayer. When we pray, many of us take on a certain posture; whether we raise our hands, kneel down, or place our hands together. We even take on a new voice and language that sounds very biblical and performed.

We make sure we say the right things and make our requests to God in a way which at times, sounds more like a business presentation than a loving relationship. In our effort to get answers, we try to persuade God to hear us and convince Him with our understanding. We let God know why He should give us the things we have requested of Him.

In reality, what the Father is looking for is that we come as sons and daughters and speak with Him in an ordinary way, expressing the desires of our hearts. He is not interested in the presentation, just that we are present. He wants the real, authentic you! (Matthew 6:7)

Once we have made our request or shared our heart, it's time to be still and rest in His presence. As we are waiting, the Father starts to speak into our heart and reveals His real self. (Again, this is often a different God than the one that others have painted.) It is in this place that you start to see revelation or understanding on how He sees the request or needs you have.

The way we see the things that we are carrying and the burdens we have are changed. That which was a problem becomes a place of heavenly possibility. As our prayer needs are offered to the Father, they take on a new reality. Sickness becomes an invitation for healing. Resistance becomes a place of breakthrough. Every need in which we see no answer is placed into the hands of a loving Father who has all the resources and power of heaven to change our circumstances. It's in this place of relational prayer that miracles are created.

The Father is not scared of the things we are going through or the needs we have. He is our Father and also the God of the universe. He has the answer and the invitation in this great relationship is for us to see how He sees and to respond how He responds. Faith is created!

For those who have enjoyed the great privilege of a good relationship with their natural father, you have some understanding of what I am talking about. In times of need, you come and share your heart with your father. He, in turn, gives you a different perspective. He speaks and reveals a way through the problem. As we listen to his heartfelt advice, we start to see the challenges we face in a different way. We see solutions and possibilities. Through conversation, our hearts are enlarged with hope.

Now, let's imagine he has unlimited resources and wisdom that defies our common sense. This is the case with our heavenly Father. Not only does He speak, which brings a different perspective, He also supplies all the resources, tools, and strategies that are required to succeed. With all this at our disposal and with all the encouragement we have received, we are ready to take action.

In this approach, you are not just praying for a need to be met. You understand the heart and nature of your heavenly Father who wants to help. Together in relationship, you come up with solutions to overcome the needs. You start to dream in a supernatural way and your prayers are answered.

Relationship and Prayer

Relationship is not one-way but requires intimacy, trust, and open hearted conversation. This creates a foundation of trust from which we believe and act.

Relationship is not about what you do and what I do. It's what we do together. The same is true of prayer. It's not what we do and then what the Father does in response, like the Old Testament, old convent position. It's what we do together. There is a conversation and response, questions and answers.

This is one of the most exciting things about being a child of God. The Father invites us to ask the deepest questions of our hearts. From experience, I know that the Father loves to answer us. Sometimes immediately, and other times over a period of time. Through our journey and relationship with Him, we always arrive at the answer and the answer is always full of revelation.

Our prayer requests open us up to a new adventure with the Father. We are often left amazed at the truths we come to understand. It is from this perspective of relationship that we have been invited to pray. That is why I have titled this book Praying with God and not Praying to God.

When we pray "to God," it becomes one dimensional. Our requests often start with what we want or need. I call these supermarket prayers. We have a list of all that we want and we go shopping or praying and expect our basket to be filled. Relational prayer is "praying with God," as the title suggests. It's the prayers that are developed when two lives or hearts have been joined together and beat as one. No longer are we asking just for the things we want, but the things that are in the heart of the Father.

Father, Abba or Daddy

As many of you know, we have been called sons and daughters. We have been adopted into the family of God. We are joint heirs with Christ Jesus. We have unlimited access to the Father or as the book of Romans describes Him, "Abba, Father." This means "daddy, Father." (Romans 8:16)

[handwritten margin note, left:] You DID all The Work

[handwritten margin note, right:] such a privilege too awesome for words

[handwritten note:] P9-41

What a wonderful description of our loving Father - Abba, Daddy! This paints a picture of a personal, loving God with an open armed invitation to us, His children. "Daddy" is a word that easily flows from the lips of His children when in play or in need. It is a word of adoration for one that we love. It is also a word we use as we cry for help in times of need. In the most difficult times, we cry "Daddy", creating a sound that rings through the heavens, waiting for a response that never fails to come.

If this is truly our position and an accurate picture of the relationship we have with our heavenly Father, then why do we often approach Him in prayer as slaves and not as sons?

Many of us cry out to God who we call Father, but we see Him as a master. We have been told the truth, that He is Abba, Daddy - Father, but we still see ourselves as slaves and not sons. As slaves, our prayer becomes a plea for mercy instead of a request of love by sons and daughters who know His heart and nature.

As slaves, we approach "the master," hoping our plea will be heard. As sons and daughters, our request is not founded in a "hope so" mentality, but in faith. We know that He hears us and delights in answering us. He loves for us to come to Him in faith, believing for that which seems impossible. He delights in responding to us then showers us with the rewards or gifts that our faith in Him has produced. (Hebrews 11:6)

A slave never feels worthy. A son knows that he has special access, rights, and inheritance. A slave is trying to please his master in order to be rewarded for his good works. A son knows that his father is already pleased with him, not because of what he has or has not done, but because of who he is in the family.

One of my favorite scriptures is when Jesus is being baptized. The Holy Spirit comes upon him and the voice of the Father is heard, "This is my beloved Son in whom I am well pleased." This statement caused me to ask why the Father was pleased with the Son. I realized that at this point, Jesus had not been in ministry or moved in signs, wonders or miracles. He had not yet achieved anything great. No one was shouting His name or declaring His great ability to preach. The Father's declaration and pleasure was not in what the Son had done, but in who the Son was. "This is my beloved Son." In the same way, the Father delights in you not because of what you have done, but because of who you are. You are a son or daughter of the king! (Luke 3:22)

Jesus told the disciples that He loved them in the same way that His Father loved Him. In this love context, Jesus also addresses the issue of slaves. He told His disciples that He no longer called them slaves, but friends, and states how this changed their relationship. As slaves, they just did what they were told to do. As friends, they were invited to know what the Master was doing. The intentions, thoughts, and even the dreams of His heart were made known to them. (John 15:9-16)

I like to imagine this with the picture of John, who is described as the disciple whom Jesus loved and lay upon His breast. (John 21:20) We, too, have been invited as friends to lay upon the breast of the Father and hear His heartbeat for other people and the burdens they have.

Another example of this relationship with the Father as friends and not slaves is seen in Moses. While everyone else stood in the doorway of his own tent, Moses would go in search of God. It is here that we see the most precious picture of relationship as "God spoke to Moses face to face as a man would speak to a friend." (Exodus 33:11)

This was Moses' starting place of prayer. He came as a friend and not as a slave. In the following verse, we see dialogue taking place in which the Father was happy to respond. (Exodus 33:12-15)

It was in this prayer relationship that the Father not only responded to Moses' request by showing him His glory, He also reveals His nature. The Lord proclaimed not just what He would do, but who He was and who He is. And the Lord passed before Moses His friend and proclaimed, "The Lord, the Lord God, merciful and gracious, longsuffering and abounding in goodness and truth." (Exodus 34:6)

This revelation would have transformed Moses' understanding as it should ours. Moses' prayer life from this day forward would change forever. No longer would he come as a slave, but as a friend. He now experienced God in His glory and power. He also came to understand the Father's heart and nature.

When we pray with God as sons and not slaves, we not only know what God is able to do, but more than that, we know what He desires to do because of His nature. We come to know the God of mercy and grace, longsuffering, abounding in goodness and truth. I don't need to question God's desire to move in our lives or upon those we would consider as undeserving. I know the heart of the Father. He proclaimed it to Moses and we have experienced His nature through the mercy and grace we have received. He loves to show mercy.

You should underline this verse and study it every day. Come to know who God is and not just what He can do, but what He will do. When we catch this revelation of the heart of the Father, it will change the way we see Him and those around us. For as God shows us mercy, so we start to pray for others with mercy. Proverbs 3:3 tell us, "Let not mercy and truth forsake you; Bind them around your neck, write them on the tablet of your heart."

When we understand the nature of the Father, it changes our prayer life. His nature reveals who He is and the motives behind what he does. We can better understand the reasons why He gives us things or why He moves in particular ways. He is more than a sugar daddy who just gives us whatever we want because He can.

Prayer becomes a place of unfolding revelation of His nature. As we learn His nature in response to our requests, it starts to lay a firm foundation for prayer. Even though God may change the way He answers our prayers, His nature is unchanging. We know God will show us mercy and grace when we have a need, but we don't necessarily know how mercy and grace will manifest in response to our need.

Let me show you how this works. Through many years of ministry, I have come across people who suddenly find themselves in a life threatening position. It may be that they have been diagnosed with a terminal disease or have been in an accident and need immediate surgery. At times, the individuals are believers and others times, they are a relative of a believer. The reality is that it doesn't really matter. God doesn't respond to our prayers based on the individual's position. God responds out of His nature.

We can stand in the gap and pray with confidence on the individual's behalf. We know that the nature of God is to show mercy and grace. We know that God will move, but what we don't know is how God will answer our pray. God may perform an instant healing that stuns the medical profession. It may be a gradual healing during which time the Holy Spirit strengthens the patient to endure the process. It may be an accelerated healing in which the individual heals much more quickly or more fully than expected. God loves to move supernaturally in people's lives, but sometimes He uses those who He has gifted as surgeons. Yes, gifted by God. After all, the Bible says "all good gifts come from the Father of lights." I have witnessed in many times of a person's need that the right surgeon turns up at just the right time. You know that one-of-a-kind surgeon. The one who specializes in the surgery you need and they just happen to be available at the time of need and are willing to operate on you. In each of these cases, the result is a reflection of God's mercy and the individual is made whole.

Prayer Driven by Love

Our prayer life should come from a position of love, not fear. Jesus said to His disciples that it was His love for them that enabled their relationship to go from slaves to friends. It's the love of the Father that invites us to pray as sons, daughters, and friends. Not as slaves. The Bible tells us that "There is no fear in love; but perfect love casts out all fear"

Our love approach to prayer reveals another aspect of the nature of the Father. Praying from a position of love and not fear is not something we start when we suddenly have a problem. This love language is first cultivated in our relationship with the Father and not just in the needs we have. It is a love that's developed in discourse and by talking face to face as a friend just as Moses talked with God. It's a love that is revealed to us as we walk and journey with the Father and He reveals a heavenly perspective of earthly things.

So, as we bring our needs to God, we quickly understand that God loves us and He loves those we love. He has given us a pair of groovy love glasses. The lenses through which we see God and the world around us have changed. For God so loved the world at its worst point and that love is infectious. As He loved and demonstrated His love by giving His only begotten Son, so we love and give and pray for those around us, even the unlovely!

When we understand His love for us, the fear we had in a situation is changed. His love firmly places us in His hands. He will not let us go to face a thing on our own. He is with us and He will never leave us. This outrageous love gives us confidence that He will answer our prayers. As we rest safely under the shadow of His wings, our fear dissipates and faith is nurtured through His love.

Not only does God love us, He loves our children. It is time to understand how God loves and sees the children we are praying for. He loves and cares for them and wants for them the very things we want and so much more. He loves to reveal to us His plans and desires for their lives. As we understand His love for them, fear dissipates, faith arises, and we know that we will have our prayers answered. What we don't know is when they will be answered.

The more we cultivate prayer as children, sons, daughters, and friends of God, the more we understand who God is. As the revelation of the Father increases in us, so the mountain before us starts to shrink. The impossible becomes possible and problems around us start to change. Our needs become subject to the power of God and we become emerged in the love and nature of God. Answers and breakthrough are released in relational prayer.

It's from this position that we, as sons and daughters, start praying. Our prayer life is transformed as we not only pray to God but we pray with God!

The Spirit Bears Witness

I want to close this chapter with what I feel is an invitation from the Father. He is a Father who cries out to His children to know Him more. And not just to know Him, but to know Him as your Father.

It may be that you have been a believer for a long time but the way you have pictured God the Father is wrong. Or maybe you are a prodigal son or daughter and you have forgotten what the Father's embrace feels like. This could be a dark season of the soul in which you feel like you have been forgotten or you feel like you are a long way from the presence of God. You may even be a great intercessor. You know how to pray and you have a great relationship with God the Father, but like any relationship, it can go to another level.

This invitation to pray is vital and foundational in understanding the rest of the Lord's Prayer. We are told that "The Spirit Himself bears witness with our spirit that we are children of God." (Romans 8:16) My prayer for you is a reflection of the heart of the Father. I desire that this prayer will become your prayer, even a daily prayer.

I pray that the Holy Spirit will touch your spirit or inner-man according to His Word. That He would bear witness with you and that you would know that you are a child of God. I pray the connection you feel today will be real, tangible, and life changing. That today you will feel like you are coming home and the Father is celebrating your return. He wants to shower you with love and gifts that are beyond your understanding. Today is the day of awakening. You are being renewed in your spirit and mind. You are receiving an upgrade in your understanding. I pray that the way you see both the Father and yourself will change through this incredible relationship that you have entered into. Let the image you have of God the Father transforms the image that you have of yourself. To know God is to know the image in which He created you when He declared, "Let us make man in our image." My prayer is that your spirit will be made alive by His Spirit who is bearing witness that the creator God is your Father and you are worthy sons and daughters through Christ Jesus.

Chapter 2: Hallowed be Your Name

In this manner, therefore, pray: Our Father in heaven, <u>Hallowed be Your name</u>. (Matthew 6.9)

When we come to God in prayer, we not only know Him as our Father, but we come to Him with an understanding of how great He is! Our hearts are filled with awe as we gaze upon all that He is and all that He has done and will do in our lives.

Much of what we read in scripture and discover in relationship with God seems to keep many truths in tension. On the one hand, God is our Father, whose arms are always open and ready to receive us however we come. We can pray anywhere and at any time with the knowledge that He is waiting for an opportunity to invade our lives with answered prayers.

On the other hand, He is a mighty God, who we come to in praise and worship. We come lifting up His name and declaring all that He is. This part of the Lord's Prayer, "Hallowed be Your name" is an act of approaching the Father in worship.

One of the greatest joys in the Christian life is to be able to come boldly before God in praise and worship. It is the act of acknowledging Him in all things and the declaration of who He is - above all things and circumstance. To worship Him is an invitation to intimately know Him and also a prophetic announcement of what He will do or who He is in our lives.

Praise is in the Name

In this place of the Lord's Prayer, we are invited to praise (hallow) His name. This is praise and worship based on His name and what His name means. This is not what we will do in our sacrifice of praise, but what He has done and who He is as discovered in the many names of God.

This is such an important truth because the answer to our prayer is not in who we are, but in who He is. Our confidence is not in man, but in our Father God. This does not mean that our prayers are always answered immediately. There will be times of being persistent in prayer where we persevere until breakthrough. But as we declare His Name in praise, we are laying a foundation of faith of who we believe God is, despite our circumstances.

The Name!

For many people, a name is just a name. When we name our children we name them after relatives as a sign of honor. We may give them a popular name, a beautiful name, or a bizarre name just to be different and to fit in with the pop culture world we live in.

As many already know, names in the Bible were not just picked, but were given by God. A name would declare a person's nature, gift, or destiny. Names had great meaning and carried a key to the individual's life.

The reason that God placed so much emphasis on a person's name was because His many names carry so much truth about who He is. His name is so much more than a title. We will use the word "God" as a title for the creator of the universe and miss the many truths of what His names declare and describe about His nature.

Israel had a different view of the names of God. They had great reverence for His names. His name was so holy that they would not use it or say it aloud. When reading the scripture, they would not say His name in full. They would spell it "YHWH" and leave out the vowels so as not to offend God. His name was too holy to get wrong.

Israel took seriously the Ten Commandment which declare, "You shall not take the name of the Lord God in vain, for the Lord will not hold him guiltless who takes His name in vain." (Exodus 20:7)

Many people today will use God's name in vain or even as a curse word, but His name is holy, full of power, and authority. His name is never a curse and is always a blessing. If we really understood the power of His name, we would also hold it in great reverence.

When God first revealed His name to Moses, who wrote the first five books of the Bible, He described His name as "I AM WHO I AM" (Exodus 3:14) This signifies that God is self-existing, self-sufficient, and the all in all.

There are so many truths that we could talk about concerning God's name and many great books have been written about this subject. My aim is to make you aware that when we approached our Father God in worship, we are to come with His name in mind. The very name that the Israelites were afraid to use, Jesus invites us to use as a key to answered prayers.

As we move through the Old Testament we see many of the names of God. Many Christians know these names because we use them as a declaration of who He is.

Some of the names of God:

> *El Shaddai – Lord God Almighty. (Genesis 17:1-3)*
>
> *El Elyon – The Most High God. (Genesis 14:18)*
>
> *Adonai – Lord, Master. (Genesis 15:2)*
>
> *Yahweh – Lord, Jehovah. (Genesis 2:4)*
>
> *Elohim – God's, as referring to the trinity. Also means God, Judge, creator. (Genesis 1:26)*
>
> *Jehovah Nissi – The Lord my Banner or the Lord my miracle. (Exodus 17:15)*
>
> *Jehovah Raah – The Lord my shepherd. (Psalm 23)*
>
> *Jehovah Rapha – The Lord that heals. (Exodus 15:26)*
>
> *Jehovah Shammah – The Lord is there. (Ezekiel 48:35)*
>
> *Jehovah Tsidkenu – The Lord our Righteousness. (Jeremiah 23:6)*
>
> *Jehovah Mekoddishkem – The Lord who sanctifies you. (Exodus 31:13)*
>
> *El Olam – The everlasting God. (Genesis 21:33)*

Qanna – Jealous or zealous. (Exodus 20:5)

Jehovah Jireh – The Lord will provide. (Genesis 22:14)

Jehovah Shalom – The Lord is peace (Judges 6:24)

Jehovah Sabaoth – The Lord of hosts or the Lord of powers. (1 Samuel 1:3)

In addition to the above names of God, we also get a better understanding of God's nature as revealed through His name when Moses has an encounter in the presence of God. In fact, God declares His name as the following:

> *Now the Lord descended in the cloud and stood with him there, and proclaimed the name of the Lord. And the Lord passed before him and proclaimed, "The Lord, The Lord God, merciful and gracious, longsuffering, and abounding in goodness and truth. (Exodus 34:5-6)*

As Moses received the revelation of God's name, he started to understand what that meant. It was more than a name, it was the way that God would interact in relationship with Moses and His people.

When we praise His name, it is not just a declaration of what God will do as an act of power. It is who He is to us. This makes it personal. God is not just "Jehovah Shalom" meaning the Lord is peace, in response to a situation. It may be that a situation moves us to pray for peace, but what God wants to do is reveal His name and therefore His nature. We declare His name as "Shalom" and peace will come into a situation. The greater work is that this prayer request has kick started our understanding of His nature. That which was an act of power in response to a need is developed by God as a lifestyle in relationship with Him.

There are many other names of God throughout the Bible in both the Old and New Testaments. We also have the many names of Jesus, our Immanuel (God with us), and the names of the Holy Spirit or the Spirit of God. All of these names carry a powerful revelation of who God is to us or in relationship with us.

When we come before God the Father in prayer, we are invited to come in worship. We declare His name and all that He is. Before we even make a request, our answer lies in His name. By worshiping and praising His name, we have already declared the solution.

This approach changes the way we see our problems, challenges, and needs. Prayer starts from an elevated position of praise. As we lift Him up by declaring His name, we are lifted up in our belief. Faith arises and our problems or mountains become smaller. Jesus said if you have a mustard seed of faith (in God) you can say to this mountain "rise up and be moved" and it shall be moved.

When we praise God by declaring His names, our mustard seed of faith is watered and hope is increased. I love the scripture in Zechariah that says:

> So he answered and said to me: "This is the word of the Lord to Zerubbabel; Not by might nor by power, but by my Spirit says the Lord of Hosts, who are you, O great mountain? Before Zerubbabel you shall become a plain! And he shall bring for the capstone with shouts of Grace, grace to it. (Zechariah 4:6-7)

When we realize who God is by declaring His name, we start to understand that God is with us. We understand that there is nothing too difficult or impossible for Him. We have praised Him and declared who He is and what He has and will do.

In praise we are re-positioned in our thinking and our faith. That which seemed impossible becomes possible, first in our hearts, and then in our lives. Our spirit man is lifted up and we know that the anointing, or power of God upon us, is greater than that which is before us.

I encourage you to declare who God is. Shout out His name in the face of the problem. It's all in His name! Speak to your mountain and see it crumble before your eyes.

King David revealed this secret in the book of Psalms:

> I will praise You, O Lord, with my whole heart: I will tell of all Your marvelous works. I will be glad and rejoice in You; I will sing praise to Your name, O Most High. When my enemies turn back, they shall fall and perish at Your presence. (Psalm 9:1-3)

King David knew that when they sang praise to His name, His name rang out in all the camp. Every warrior declared in unison the name of God. In both the ears of Israel and their enemy, His name was a declaration of God's intention.

Thanksgiving

When we come to the Father in worship and lift His name, it brings us to a place of thanksgiving, regardless of the circumstances.

The scriptures says:

> Enter into His gates with thanksgiving, and into His courts with praise, be thankful to Him, and bless His <u>name</u>. (Psalm 100:4)

When life is tough it's easy to come before God complaining and moaning about all that we are struggling with. The children of Israel learned that this was not the best way to approach God or to receive the blessings of God. In fact, their moaning and complaining caused them to remain in the wilderness for forty years. A whole generation missed out on the greater blessings of God and they failed to inherit the Promised Land. Israel had to discover a better way of moving forward other than moaning and complaining!

The enemy loves for us to be fixated on the problem because it blinds us to the solution. He loves for us to moan and complain because in it, there is no peace or hope. It steals our vision and undermines the promises of God.

God is our answer in the midst of the problem. When we stop accusing Him and start thanking Him for who He is, our outlook changes. Thanksgiving changes the lens through which we see God and the world around us. We stop reducing God to the size of our problem and the problem is reduced in the presence of our God.

The source of our thanksgiving is in His name. As we saw earlier, God declared His name to Moses and in that, described Himself as good! (Exodus 34:5-6)

We know that we serve a good God and a good Father. He will not leave us alone in our mess. He will meet us there. He is often just waiting for an invitation.

There is a great picture of Jesus, who is a reflection of the Father, saving a young woman from the mess she was in. We read that this woman had been caught in adultery. The Jewish leaders brought her before Jesus hoping that He, too, would condemn her. Many of us know the story. Jesus responds with grace – the nature of our Father. He did not judge her, but gave her a way through her mess. Jesus invited her accusers to stone her if they had never sinned themselves. They could not because all have sinned and fallen short of the grace of God. In the middle of the discussion, Jesus knelt down and wrote in the sand with His finger. Just take a moment and imagine the picture. The woman who was cast into the dirt was met by Jesus kneeling down in the dirt with one intention, to lift her out. Jesus will step into our mess and lift us out of it.

We are encouraged to give thanks to God in every situation:

> In everything give thanks; for this is the will of God in Christ Jesus for you. (1 Thessalonians 5:18)

Even in times of sickness and difficulty, we should thank God. We are not thanking God for the illness and obstacles themselves, but in spite of them. We are to thank Him in every situation because we know that He will "turn all things for good." He is already working on our behalf. His name and all that His name declares He is will be established in our tests. Our tests will become a testimony that again reveal His name and nature!

When we give thanks, our unsettled nervous heart, emotions, and fears in a situation will be transformed into a place of peace.

Be anxious for nothing but in everything by prayer and supplication with thanksgiving let your requests be made known to God: and the peace of God, which surpasses all understanding, will guard your hearts and minds through Christ Jesus. (Philippians 4:6-7)

Many people come to prayer out of a place of fear. Life's circumstances start to control the way they think. Thanksgiving transforms our approach and prayer life. It changes our language. We start to speak words of life instead of death. We prophesy who God is and therefore what He will do. Where our lives were once riddled with anxiety, we find hope and peace in God.

Weapon of Warfare

Praise and worship is a great weapon of warfare. It is often the difference between winning and losing a battle.

One of the names of God is Jehovah Nissi. This name means "The Lord my Banner, the Lord my miracle or the Lord my conquest." (Exodus 17:15) Moses used this name of God to describe His name over the children of Israel. It was a name that meant God would be with them in battle or conquest and bring them victory. It was a declaration that they were on the winning side because God was with them.

As believers, we will go through many battles. It is what or who you exult within the battle that you will give power to. If we look at sickness without the revelation of the Jehovah Rapha (The Lord our healer), we will give power to the sickness. If we give thanks to and exult Jehovah Rapha, we remove the sting of sickness and start to trust in God our healer. The problems we face become the source of a supernatural solution.

Paul said it like this:

> *For though we walk in the flesh, we do not war according to the flesh. For the weapons of our warfare are not carnal but mighty in God for the pulling down of strongholds, casting down arguments and every high thing that <u>exalts</u> itself against the knowledge of God, bringing every thought into captivity to obedience of Christ. (2 Corinthians 10:3-5)*

This is fascinating! Every thought, imagination, and lie of the devil is trying to derail your faith. These lies exalt themselves against the knowledge of Christ. If we take the bait, we will start to believe the lies and by doing so, we exalt or lift up the problem. We make the problem greater than the truth. We reduce the name of God and lift up a false god – which is the lie, the imagination, or problem.

Once we realize what we are dealing with and change our declaration and start to exalt the name of God, the problem and lies are reduced. They come into the obedience of Christ. We are left with the question, who is Christ in your situation? What has He done and what will He do in you and for you?

The same is said of the Father. When we come to "Our Father in Heaven" with a shout of praise, "Hallowed be Your Name" we choose to exalt Him. We lift up His name, Jehovah Nissi, as a banner and the one who brings our conquest. The problem becomes a possibility and a place for a miracle.

Praising with God

Praising with God is a great interactive picture of praise and worship with our Father God. As we start to declare who He is, we start to see who we are.

As we lift up the many names of God; like healer, provider, and banner, we understand who God is and we see Him as the great "I AM WHO I AM." The reflection that comes from who God is in himself is who He becomes to us. If He is healer, the reflection is that we are healed. If He is provider, then we are provided for. If God is our banner, then we will see breakthrough and victory in battle.

God does not suddenly become something in response to our need. God already exists as the solution and invites us to come to Him as the answer. Who God is has already been established by His name.

> But without faith it is impossible to please Him, for he who comes to God must believe that He is and that He is a rewarder of those who diligently seek Him. (Hebrews 11:6)

Some may struggle with this next thought because your relationship with the Father may be different from mine. I believe that in the same way that God calls us to pray *with* Him in relationship and not just *to* Him, so too does He invite us to worship *with* Him and not just *to* Him.

In daily life, I love to make up songs with my daughter, Addalynn. I will sing over her all kinds of things. I will tell her of my love and who she is to me. In response, she does the same and sings who I am to her. She will mirror the songs and thoughts that I am proclaiming over her.

This is similar to our relationship with and worship of the Father. It is not that the Father is worshiping us, but He is singing over us and our response is to mirror His love and worship the Father. We know that the Father sings over us because the Bible tells us that He does:

> *The Lord your God in your midst, The mighty one will save; He will rejoice over you with gladness. He will quiet you with His love. He will rejoice over you with singing. (Zephaniah 3:17)*

Some may struggle to imagine God singing over them in a way that creates a response. We know that He is always proclaiming who we are. The Spirit of God is always bearing witness to us as children of God. It says that we are joint heirs with Christ and therefore we have a great inheritance. (Romans 8:17-17)   P9, 21

God sings over us and maybe we hear just a whisper in our hearts of how He sees us. His songs are prophetic in nature; they declare who we are becoming. They create a picture that is often opposite to our circumstances and it produces a reaction from us. As we hear His songs, words, or rejoicing, it causes us to make a shout of praise or song from our hearts to His heart. God sings over us out of the storehouse of His abundant love. We respond out of the love we have received.

When we lift the name of God, we are bringing Glory to His name. The reflection is that we are impacted by the glory of who He is. We start to reflect His name and glory as a mirror.

> *But we all, with unveiled face, behold as in a mirror the glory of the Lord, are being transformed into the same image from glory to glory, just as by the Spirit of the Lord. (2 Corinthians 3:18)*

When you come to God the Father in prayer, start to worship and declare who God is as proclaimed in His name. You cannot help but be moved by this and soon you will receive what you have in Him because of who He is in you.

Many of you already know the story of Gideon and how God called him. It was during a time in which Israel had been under an ongoing assault from the Midianites. For seven years, they had been under attack with many casualties and the loss of their harvests.

Gideon was a man who was hiding in a winepress. God visited him and called him out of hiding. He had been chosen as the next judge in Israel. Like many judges, he was to be their deliverer. He was the answer to the problem.

As we know, Gideon did not have the same vision or perspective of himself that God had of him. He was struggling with his faith and wondered why God had not shown up in a way that he had thought God would. Gideon had heard reports and stories of what God had done in the past. However, at this time in his life, there seemed to be no sign of God or at least the God he had heard about.

Like many of us, God chose Gideon in his weakness. He called him in the midst of his questions and declared promises over him that were very different than the man who stood before Him.

Gideon realized that God was serious about choosing him. In response, he brings a sacrifice as an act of worship. Gideon still had questions and challenges in front of him. The war was still raging and Gideon was still the reluctant deliverer, but this was his worship.

This act of sacrifice was his prayer, praise, or "hallowed be Your name". Once Gideon brought his sacrifice to God, it was consumed by fire. His worship was accepted and God started to speak to him. God loves to meet us in our sacrifice. This is what God said and Gideon's response:

Then the Lord said to him, peace be with you, do not fear, you shall not die. So Gideon built an altar, and called it The-Lord-is-peace. (Jehovah Shalom) To this day it is still in Ophrah of the Abiezrites. (Judges 6:23-24)

When God spoke to Gideon, He revealed Himself in the midst of the battle and declared His own name as the God of peace. This is something very different than that which Israel was facing. Israel was facing war and chaos, but God was peace. Gideon gets hold of this revelation and declares the name of the Lord as Jehovah Shalom – The Lord is peace!

Even before the victory, Gideon understood the name of the Lord. This was the altar he built upon the name of God, before the victory that was won. This was his praise before he had a praise report.

We know the rest of the story, or so we think! Gideon comes under the anointing of the Holy Spirit. His army is reduced to three hundred men. After receiving a word from the Lord, he goes into battle and gains a great victory. The battle was not his. The victory was not because he was a great warrior, but because God was with him. In fact, God told him that He reduced Gideon's army so he would always know that it was God who brought the victory.

After the Midianites were defeated, the scripture declares that it was quiet or they <u>had peace</u> for forty years. (Judges 8:28)

Gideon got hold of God's name and declared it, "hallowed" it, before he saw it (peace) come to pass. God responded to His name and not only brought victory, but also brought peace instead of war. He established peace for forty years.

When we come to the Father, we are invited to come and worship Him by name. As He invites us to declare His name, so we invite Him to establish His name. As we lift up His name, His name becomes the foundation of our breakthrough and testimony.

Chapter 3: Your Kingdom Come

Your kingdom come. *Your will be done. On earth as it is in heaven. (Matthew 6:10)*

This next area of the Lord's Prayer is a wonderful invitation and at times a scary reality. As we come to understand what we are asking for in "Your kingdom come," we realize that we are praying a prayer of surrender; a prayer that invites God's kingdom to come and invade our world.

This is exciting from the point of view that we come to have a supernatural expectation. Our lives and destiny are not just dependent on what we see in the natural, but on what takes place in the hidden realm of God's kingdom.

We understand that our world is not just subject to the laws of nature, but also to the laws of God. In fact, the first law that God established was not natural, but supernatural. In the book of Genesis we read that God created the heaven and the earth and God said "Let there be light." He called the light into being out of darkness. It was the Word of God that created something out of nothing. The light did not come about by natural laws, but by supernatural power and the word that proceeded out of the mouth of God.

As believers we are not only living in a natural world, but a supernatural kingdom. It's from this place that we invite a supernatural God to invade our world and change our natural realm by His supernatural presence.

The laws of the kingdom are not bound by the laws of this world. The natural laws of this world are subject to the kingdom of God and the supernatural. The kingdom of God has power beyond the natural. This is why when Jesus came preaching the kingdom, He also demonstrated the power of the kingdom with signs and wonders. This is how He was able to heal the sick and cast out demons. He was not operating under the laws of the natural, but under the authority and power of the kingdom of God.

The natural laws of this world suggest that the only way a problem can be solved is with a natural solution. For example, the only hope for the sick is the medicine that a doctor prescribes.

We cannot ignore the natural laws and we know that they are effective for many people. However, as believers, our hope and future is not just bound by the natural. This is an exciting prospect. We serve in a different kingdom that has different, supernatural realities.

There is a woman in the Bible who was desperate and came looking for Jesus. Many have read her story about the blood condition she had for twelve years. She had spent all of her money on doctors without finding a solution. After all of her searching, she still had the condition.

Just to make this clear, I am not against doctors or the medical profession. They have been gifted by God to do what they do and to bring answers and hope to many people. Jesus did not rebuke the woman for going to the doctor, He just had a solution that the doctors did not offer. This solution was based in the kingdom He represented.

When the woman grabbed hold of Jesus' garment in both desperation and faith, she got her answer. The natural gave way to the supernatural power that was at work in and through Jesus. The condition she had suddenly changed. In a moment, she was healed and restored.

When we pray let "Your kingdom come," we are inviting the Father to release all of the promises and power of heaven to invade our lives and the world we live in. We are not only yielding our needs, but we are also surrendering our reliance on the natural laws of this world for an answer. We have an expectation for God to move in a supernatural way.

I like the way King David describes this in the book of Psalms:

> *My soul waits silently for God alone, For my expectation is from Him. He alone is my rock and my salvation; He is my defense: I shall not be moved. (Psalm 62:5-6)*

When we have an expectation that God will come with His kingdom, we rest in a knowledge that there is an answer even when we can't see it. It gives us freedom from anxiety and worry and we learn to wait on God. Our soul, emotions, and heart come to a place of rest. Our expectation declares the promises of God who is our rock, our salvation, and our defense.

The part of this Psalm I love the most is when it declares and shouts from the page, "I shall not be moved." There are many things we face in life that so easily interfere with our hope. With a kingdom mindset, our outlook is full of the expectation of His coming kingdom. We are no longer double minded in our opinion and faith. As described in the book of James, we are no longer tossed about by every thought or wind of doctrine. Our expectation in God has set the tone and in this truth, hope is restored and I will not be moved!

Our supernatural expectation sets our feet upon the rock. The waves still crash and storms of life still rage around us. Our footing may even feel unsteady at times as the waves crash over the rock upon which we stand. But once the storm is done and the waves have rolled back, our feet remain steady upon our rock, Jesus!

In life, I live with an expectation that God is going to speak or show up in a way that will blow my mind. I expect to see God move in a supernatural way every day. His kingdom is real and my prayer is an invitation for it to change my world.

Building the Kingdom, not Castles

This is the part that can be slightly scary because we like to be in control. We live in a world in which we determine what we do and when we do it, or so we think. It is only when the unexpected happens that we truly realize that we are not as in control as we thought. Out of pride, we will try to find our own solution to problems, but humility invites help from God.

As an English man I understand the saying, "a man's home is his castle." Having grown up in a land of castles, I have seen many of them throughout the country. These fortified structures are built to keep any invading kingdom out. At the same time, they provide comfort for the family or families that live in them. The castles of old were governed by the king of the castle.

Historically, the way of life inside the various castles was lived according to the word or the laws of the king. Every castle had different laws and lifestyles according to the king of the castle.

No castle can have more than one king. If another king comes to the castle, they are not king of that castle. They are subject to the king that owns or governs the castle they have visited. They are king of another kingdom, but not this one. That is, unless the visiting king invades the castle and removes the resident king. If this takes place, the laws and life of the castle are now subject to a new king who rules with different laws and a new way of thinking.

There can never be more than one ruling king governing a given castle. If there were two kings in one castle, the kingdom would be in conflict. There would be confusion among the people as to which king to follow. It would bring uncertainty about which laws should be observed and who the people should serve. This castle would no longer offer security to those who live within its walls. It would be a kingdom in chaos and open to attack.

When we make the statement that "a man's home is his castle", we are declaring that we are "king of the castle." There is no space or room for another king. The way we live and the rules we live by have been set and no outside force will change them. All the plans for ruling and reigning are in our hands. We will decide how our home and family will be governed. It is in our own hands to manage our affairs and family. We will defend our principles and overcome the obstacles of life.

I am sure you can see the challenge when we pray the Lord's Prayer and invite "Your Kingdom to come." Every kingdom has a king with dominion, which is where we get the word "king-dom" from. This can be better described as "king with dominion". When we pray the

Lord's Prayer, we are surrendering our castle to His kingdom and to a greater king. After all, Jesus is the King of kings. There cannot be more than one king in a castle. So for Jesus to rule and reign in our lives with supernatural power, we have to surrender our rights as king of our castle.

This changes everything in the way we live. We are no longer governed by the old man or the old way of thinking, but by the new man in Christ. Transformation takes place. Our rules are now subject to His Word. We place our dreams and desires into His hands and take on His purposes and plans for our lives. This changes our destiny in a wonderful way. The exciting part is that His kingdom comes with much more power and influence than ours. Our castle is no longer subject just to the laws of nature, but the supernatural power of His kingdom. The outlook is bright but first we have to yield control.

I love the prayer, "Your kingdom come" but I don't always like the process of letting go. However, every time you surrender something to God, you will be amazed at how He works and moves in those areas of your life.

In the natural, we would think that by praying this prayer we are just subjects and slaves to another king. This is only part of the truth. The kingdom of God is different than the kingdoms of this world. As we have already discussed and will see a little later in chapter 5, we are not slaves, but sons and daughters of the King.

We have not just been called to carry out the commands of a king, but we have become joint heirs in the kingdom to work in relationship with the King of kings. The reality is that we become a part of the most exciting family and kingdom in which nothing is too difficult or impossible for Him, and therefore, for us.

Seek First the Kingdom

Praying "Your kingdom come" is put into context by a statement that Jesus made to his disciples. This is best understood when we see it through the eyes of relationship with our heavenly Father.

> *".... For your heavenly Father knows that you need all these things But seek first the kingdom of God and His righteousness, and all these things will be added to you."* (Matthew 6:32b - 33)

In this scripture, Jesus was talking about the things that people worry about; the everyday stuff like food and clothing. How many of us have wondered how we will get through the week or pay our latest bill? We all have issues that consume us and cause us concern.

Jesus tells us that the Father already knows what you need. He is not blind to our needs and He has a solution already in place. The answer to our problem seems disjointed. Jesus suggests we take our eyes off the need and place it on the kingdom. We need to change our view, our lenses, or the problem we are transfixed on. This seems strange because you would think that if we lose sight of the problem, it will never be resolved. Like most challenges, the need consumes us. It actually blurs our vision. The more we look at it, the bigger the problem becomes. The moment we yield the need to God and focus on the kingdom, we relinquish control. God takes up the need and while we are concentrating on the kingdom, He is working in the background to bring a supernatural solution.

Sometimes our prayers are full of what "I want" and what "I need" which causes us to miss the things He wants for us and how He wants to use us. The "I" builds our castle and not His kingdom. There may be great things ahead of us, but our focus is set upon the need we currently have. We are stuck in the "me" mess and it stops us from seeing the greater plans and purposes of God. Let's be real, God already has an answer for us. As long as we are fixed on the problem, we will miss out on the blessings.

When we focus on the kingdom and what God wants, our needs are always met. This is kingdom thinking and it is different from the way we would normally think. When Jesus sent the disciples on a mission, He instructed them to preach the gospel of the kingdom and demonstrate the power of the kingdom by healing the sick and casting out demons. He also told them that they could not take silver or gold with them. He wanted them to learn that when they did the will of the Father, their personal needs would be met. (Matthew 10:1-16)

There will be times in our lives and ministries when we will have needs and we will ask God to intervene. God's solution may seem strange at times. For example, we may be struggling with an area of sickness, but He will have us start praying for someone else who is sick. Or, we will have a financial need and God will instruct us to give the little we have to help another. This doesn't make natural sense but this is kingdom thinking. As we take our eyes off of ourselves and seek first the kingdom, so our needs are met. As we sow into another person's life, we will reap a harvest in our own lives.

To "seek <u>first</u> the kingdom," literally means to put the kingdom and the things of God above and before the things we want. Our invitation in "Your kingdom come" is surrendering our first choice and desire of what we want in exchange for what He wants for us or through us.

In my experience, every time I put the kingdom first, the blessings upon my life far outweigh the needs I have or the things I would have requested.

When the Opposite is More Real

The kingdom of God is so different from the kingdoms of this world in both power and understanding. The way we see things in the natural is not the way that God sees those same things. What we see as a disadvantage or problem, God sees as an opportunity for the kingdom to be made manifest.

One day, Jesus goes to the top of a mountain and starts to teach the disciples about the kingdom and what it looks like. In every statement He made about the way the kingdom of God impacts people lives, He reveals the way we see life and the way the same lives are viewed in the kingdom.

When we pray "Your kingdom come", we are inviting heaven to bring a greater revelation or understanding of who we are. We are asking God to redefine how we see the circumstances we are in or the challenges we face. God's world view is different from our world view until we are transformed and have a renewed mind and start to think more like God. The Father works from the position of your potential and who you are in His kingdom and not from the position of your circumstances. We know this discussion as the beatitudes:

Then He opened His mouth and taught them, saying:

"Blessed are the poor in spirit,
For theirs is the kingdom of heaven.
Blessed are those who mourn,
For they shall be comforted.
Blessed are the meek,
For they shall inherit the earth.
Blessed are those who hunger and thirst for righteousness,
For they shall be filled.

Blessed are the merciful,
For they shall obtain mercy.
Blessed are the pure in heart,
For they shall see God.
Blessed are the peacemakers,
For they shall be called sons of God.
Blessed are those who are persecuted for righteousness'
sake,
For theirs is the kingdom of heaven.
Blessed are you when they revile and persecute you, and say
all kinds of evil against you falsely for My sake.
Rejoice and be exceedingly glad, for great is your reward in
heaven, for so they persecuted the prophets who were
before you." (Matthew 5:2-12)

How does this change your prayers? This gives you a new vision or a new set of lenses. That which was out of focus now becomes clear. Your natural understanding of how you see your life is changed by a kingdom reality. When you pray, you start to seek God from a kingdom perspective of hope and not our former, depressing view of hopelessness.

Anointed Kings of the Kingdom

In the Old Testament we read about those who were chosen as kings. They had to be anointed with oil. The oil represents the Holy Spirit who would come upon the kings and enable them to rule their kingdom in an extraordinary way. Their ability as king to rule successfully was not in their own natural ability. In fact, King Saul saw himself as the least of his tribe and King David was a shepherd boy. They did not have the right qualifications to be kings. What they had was the anointing of the Holy Spirit and a reliance on a supernatural God to lead them.

Jesus came as the king of the kingdom of God. He was also anointed, not with oil, but with the Holy Spirit. It was at His baptism that the anointing of the Holy Spirit was seen upon Him and the Father spoke from heaven declaring that Jesus was His Son.

Jesus was led into the wilderness for forty days. It was during this time that His authority was established. He was tested by the devil and overcame every temptation. The battle is not meant to defeat you, but to establish you under the anointing.

After this, Jesus returned in the power of the Holy Spirit to His hometown of Nazareth. It was here that He went into the synagogue and found the place in the book of Isaiah and started to read.

> *"The Spirit of the LORD is upon Me,*
> *Because He has anointed Me*
> *To preach the gospel to the poor;*
> *He has sent Me to heal the brokenhearted,*
> *To proclaim liberty to the captives*
> *And recovery of sight to the blind,*
> *To set at liberty those who are oppressed; To proclaim the*
> *acceptable year of the LORD." (Luke 4:18-19)*

It is important for us to continually read this and remind ourselves of what the anointed king of the kingdom brings. When the king comes, things change. The natural gives way to the kingdom. The brokenhearted are healed, captives are set free, and the blind see. The king comes with liberty and freedom for those who are oppressed.

When we read Isaiah 61 from where this scripture has been taken, we read so much more of what the king of the kingdom brings. We read that God will give us beauty instead of ashes, joy instead of mourning, praise instead of heaviness (Isaiah 61:3) and double honor instead of shame. (Isaiah 61:7)

When the King of the kingdom comes, He comes with an opposite spirit than that which we are experiencing in life. This is reflected in both this scripture and the beatitudes. What we see as a dead-end or obstacle, He sees as an open door. What we observe as a season of trial and tribulation, He sees as a time in which we are being forged in a furnace. We are being prepared and perfected for an upgrade or promotion. The giant in front of you is the stepping stone to your destiny. Your present battle is not to defeat you, but to establish you as a warrior and overcomer. Our need for provision is His opportunity to reveal His nature as provider and His promise to meet your needs.

Jesus doesn't want us to rest in our difficult circumstances; He came to violently change them.

> *"... for this reason the Son of God was manifests, that He might destroy the works of the devil. (1 John 3:8)*

Jesus demonstrated this when He was woken out of a peaceful sleep in the midst of a storm. The disciples were afraid. They thought they were going to die and they didn't know what to do so they woke Jesus up from His peaceful sleep. Jesus responds by violently rebuking the demonic storm and it became still; almost as if it never happened. (Mark 4:35-41)

The peace that Jesus was experiencing in His personal journey was extended to those around Him. This is a great picture of the kingdom that Jesus experienced in His own life. It's also interesting that Jesus reveals that we can both be at peace and violently rebuke the enemy. The kingdom within us is so powerful that we speak not from a place of fear, but faith. Instead of stealing our peace, what we see in the natural is impacted by what we know in our hearts.

The environment you live in has been created by the way you think or live. It has been influenced by your emotions and beliefs. It carries a response to the words you speak. Everyone who comes into your space is impacted by the environment that has been created. The environment is like your castle and in the case of the storm, the disciples had created an environment of fear. It was a toxic place and effected everyone in the storm.

Then we see Jesus in the midst of the storm. He lived out of a different way of thinking. His rule and reign was not subject to the demonic storm, but had greater power over the storm. When they woke Jesus up, they were inviting Him to invade their castle of thought, imagination, and the world they lived in. Jesus had a different belief system. He cultivated a world that operated out of peace and not fear. Yet, His peace had the power to rebuke the storm. The words Jesus spoke, "Peace be still", came out of a kingdom environment in which He lived and operated.

Praying "Your kingdom come" is not a weak prayer of surrender. We do not pray it because we have no other hope or are out of options. It's an empowered prayer full of possibilities. It's a prayer of expectation and trust in God. It's a cry that comes from the revelation that our natural world is about to give way to a kingdom that's full of power. It's a prayer that functions out of peace and trust in God and not out of fear. Get ready; things are about to get interesting.

The Kingdom and God Adventures

Every time we pray "Your kingdom come", we go on a new journey. If you are like me, you like to know every challenge and difficulty at the start of a journey so you can be prepared for what you will face. However, that's not possible because it's a journey or road that you may not have been on before and the kingdom manifests itself in many different ways.

I think this journey is better described as a new adventure with God. This area of prayer will take you to new places of discovery. Journeying with God is like an Indiana Jones adventure. You never know what's going to take place or what you will discover while going after the prize. It's during the adventure that we discover something new about God and ourselves.

The challenges we face or adventures we go on are an opportunity for God to show up in a miraculous way. It creates those "wow" moments of breakthrough that are undeserved. It's an adventure that is subject to His rule and reign and the supernatural laws of the kingdom of heaven!

Chapter 4: Your Will Be Done

Your kingdom come. <u>Your will be done.</u> On earth as it is in heaven. (Matthew 6:10)

I am sure you are like me and want your prayers answered. I want to know that when I pray, God will hear me and respond. I don't want to shoot off a dozen prayers hoping that one finds its way into the heart of God. I want to hit the target and know that we are on the same page. Are there any guarantees? Can I be confident that God will hear and answer my prayers?

To both of these questions, there is a resounding "yes!" We can be confident and know that God will answer our prayers. The secret or revelation (because God does not want to hide it from you, but wants to reveal His secrets to you) is found in two areas. First, His "will be done" starts with His "kingdom come" and not our kingdom. Secondly, it's in the understanding that we can know His will and pray with precision.

Not My Will

In this first area, we may be asking for guidance in what we should do or what God wants to do in our lives. It's the willingness to lay down our own wants and desires and seek God's purpose for our lives.

Jesus prayed this prayer in the garden of Gethsemane just before He was arrested. As He wrestled with that which was before Him and His death upon the cross, He knew what he had to do, but the journey was painful. He prayed:

> *He went a little further and fell on His face, and prayed, saying, "O my Father, if it is possible, let this cup pass from Me; nevertheless, not as I will but as You will." (Matthew 26:39)*

In this prayer, He expressed that if there was another way, He would take it. If it was possible to do it differently, He would have. However, He knew that this was not a prayer that the Father would answer. The salvation of all mankind hung upon His decision to fulfill the will of the Father in redeeming His children. There was no other way. Therefore, Jesus surrendered His will to the will of the Father.

The immediate future looked bleak; full of pain and death, but the rewards were eternal. His obedience brought life and freedom.

> *Looking unto Jesus, the author and finisher of our faith, who for the joy that was set before Him endured the cross, despising shame, and has sat down at the right hand of the throne of God. (Hebrews 12:2)*

There are times when it seems easier to do what we want. We all have a will and desire but it is in surrender that we see prayers answered.

When we do what we want, we operate in pride. We think we know best. God resists the proud and gives grace to the humble. (1 Peter 5:5) When we do the will of God, we get the backing of heaven. When we do what God wills, we know, without question or hesitation, that He will also open the doors and make the way for us to fulfill His purposes.

Knowing the Will of God

Knowing the will of God is a sure way of seeing our prayers answered. It also positions us to pray with God and not just to God. If we know what He wants, we are praying from a place of relationship as sons and not just slaves.

> Now this is the confidence that we have in Him, that if we ask anything according to His will, He hears us. And if we know that He hears us, whatever we ask, we know that we have the petitions that we have asked of Him. (1 John 5:14-15)

When we pray the will of God, we are able to pray confidently or with great boldness. We can ask knowing and being assured that God hears us. We come boldly into the throne room of grace knowing that we have an audience with our Father.

There is something about the will of God that deposits faith. We are not crossing our fingers and hoping God hears us. We know that He is listening and is ready to answer. I am sure there are times when God is just waiting for an invitation or for you to say the word. God will not cross over into your will. Even Jesus said, "Behold I stand at the door and knock." He is waiting for the invitation to come in. God has given us free will to do as we choose. But, the moment we surrender our will and pray His will, we open the door for the kingdom to come on earth as it is in heaven.

I find this kind of funny. The scripture says you can ask "anything" with confidence of an answered prayer. Then it qualifies the "anything" as according to His will. This means that not every prayer we pray will be answered. The Bible says that we can "pray a miss." Maybe you want something, but it's not in the will of God for you to have it. It may be dangerous for you or may lead you astray. When we pray the will of God, there is no option but for God to answer our prayers. It is guaranteed!

When we pray His will, the desires of our hearts actually start in the heart of the Father. Like John who laid upon the breast of Jesus, we are invited to lie upon and hear the heartbeat of the Father. His will becomes our passion. Our passion turns into a confident prayer and this starts a new adventure with God.

The apostle John who wrote about praying with the "will of God" in mind also demonstrated this when he prayed the following:

> Beloved, I pray that you may prosper in all things and be in health, just as your soul prospers. (3 John 2)

John would not have prayed this prayer so confidently if he did not know that it was the will of God. He caught hold of God's desire to prosper us in all things. This prosperity and health did not start with silver and gold but in the health of our soul.

The problem that most people have is not their inability to pray or lack of desire to call out to God in times of need. They struggle to have confidence that God will hear them. The foundation of the request should start in the will of God. Perhaps you can look at it this way; if you have a need, ask the Holy Spirit to reveal to you the heart of God in the matter. How does God see the issue? What does the need look like if we place Jesus in the middle of it? How would He speak into the challenge that is before you?

As both a pastor and conference speaker, I have asked God on many occasions to open doors for ministry. I only want to walk through the doors He opens. I know that when He opens a door, there is a kingdom purpose and great things will happen. While praying this prayer one morning, I clearly heard the Holy Spirit speak to me. He said, "You pray for open doors but I have called you to be a key and open doors for others." I instantly knew the will of the Father. His desire was that I would help unlock areas of ministry or doors for other people. I knew that God wanted me to activate the gifts He had given to others.

> "Counsel (purpose) in the heart of man is like deep water, But a man of understanding will draw it out." (Proverbs 20:5)

I have seen on many occasions when ministering in new areas or churches that miracles would take place and breakthrough would come. The Apostolic anointing upon my life is to bring breakthrough. The supernatural breakthrough is not to establish my ministry, but to establish other people in the kingdom. It's not to bring an answer to my prayers as much as to bring an answer to their prayers.

From that day forward, my prayer in this area has changed. No longer do I ask for open doors. I pray the will of the Father; that He would send me to places that I can be used as a key to unlock the kingdom of God in other people's lives, churches, and ministries.

We see this kind of prayer taking place in the book of Acts. Jesus tells his disciples that they are going to receive the power of the Holy Spirit. The purpose of the power was so that they would be effective witnesses of Jesus. They were to preach the gospel In Jerusalem, Judea, Samaria, and to the ends of the earth. (Acts 1:8)

The instruction and will of the Father was clear, but after a period of time, they find themselves in the middle of a spiritual storm. The disciples had been obedient and proclaimed the kingdom of God. This resulted in the power of the kingdom being released. It invaded earth and the sick were healed. The religious people started getting upset at what they were seeing. Perhaps they were afraid because they couldn't contain or control this phenomenon and so they arrested Peter and John for preaching the gospel.

When they were eventually released from prison, they were given strict orders to stop speaking about Jesus. Upon leaving with their orders, they met with the other disciples. Together, they prayed. Their prayer was not influenced by fear, but by the will of God. They knew where they had been called to and what they were to do. There was no option to run or leave town.

The disciples prayed in response to the threats they had received, but with the will of God in mind. They did not ask for a way of escape because they knew this prayer would not be answered. So they prayed to receive another impartation of the Holy Spirit. They asked for more of the very thing that got them in trouble in the first place.

God answered their prayers because they prayed for "His kingdom to come, His will be done." Not only did the disciples receive another impartation of the Holy Spirit, they were given greater boldness. They began to preach the Word of God in great power. The grace, or the empowering anointing of the Holy Spirit, was upon them in a greater measure. (Acts 4)

Prophetic Prayer

At times, we have all prayed out of need. Something comes up, we panic, and run into the arms of God where we are met by His grace.

We have all experienced God's grace in receiving answered prayers to our cries of panic. However, if our prayer life is only molded in times of great need, true relationship is never developed.

How much better would our prayer life be if we knew the will of God through prophetic insight? What if prayer started with us knowing the heart or mind of God in a situation we are facing before we started praying? If we knew His will, we would cultivate relational prayer. This would cause us to pray with God and not just to God.

Prophetic prayer opens dialogue and gives greater insight. It doesn't start with a cry for God to intervene, but a question of what God is doing or what God wants to do in a given situation. Prayer becomes a working relationship; interaction between heaven and earth. Our prayer life becomes a place where we are first receiving instruction or vision before we partner with God in prayer. This kind of prayer releases answers and breakthrough that have been guided by the will of the Father.

One of the ways of knowing the will of God is through prophecy. This may be a word that someone shares with you and it gives you hope in a present situation. It could also be a word that speaks into your life, family, business, or calling for a time in the future.

The prophetic is also when God speaks directly to us and unlocks a promise for our present or future life in Christ. We catch hold of the word and it creates faith in the journey or on our adventure with God. We know that what He has spoken is His will. This leads us to pray confidently.

The apostle Paul encouraged Timothy to use the prophecies that were spoken over him. He was to use them as a weapon of warfare. Prophecies are a weapon in our hands, hearts, and mouths. They carry with them the heart of God. No matter what we face, God has already given us a glimpse into His future.

The prophecies spoken over Timothy would stir faith within him when everything or everyone seemed to oppose the will of God in his life. The same is true for us. No matter what we see in the natural, there is a different story being written with God the Father as the author. There is a surprise ending for those who are looking at our situation from the outside. For those of us who have received prophetic insight, we are not surprised. We have already read or seen the end of the matter.

This is what Paul said to Timothy:

> "This charge I commit to you, son Timothy, according to the prophecies previously made concerning you, that by them you may wage the good warfare. Having faith and a good conscience, which some having rejected, concerning the faith have suffered shipwreck. (1 Timothy 2:18-19)

Often, what we are facing on earth looks very different to what God has promised in heaven. As sure as the earth is subject to the heavens, so our circumstances are subject to the words of God. As we take hold of His words, we are laying hold of His will. In this we can have extreme confidence that what has been spoken will come to pass.

The prophetic injects extraordinary faith into our prayer life. We stop pleading with God out of desperation and seek God out of assured hope.

"Now faith is the substance of things hoped for, the evidence of things not seen." (Hebrews 11:1)

After the resurrection, Jesus met with the disciples and gave them an important assignment. He told them to wait in Jerusalem. (Acts 1:4) Now, that doesn't seem very exciting, but there are times when God does more in the waiting than in the running after something. It was a time for them to rest. However, this rest was not in inactivity, but in expectation.

The will of God for them to "wait" came with a promise of the baptism of the Holy Spirit who would be poured out upon them on the day of Pentecost. (Acts 1:8) They heard the words Jesus said and responded. They waited. They had a glimpse of what would happen. They knew in part or in promise without ever experiencing exactly what was about to take place. I am sure they were amazed when it actually happened, but Peter knew "This was that, which was written in the book of Joel."

In their waiting, we find the disciples along with the women and Mary, the mother of Jesus, meeting for prayer. Before they received the promise, they continued together with one accord in prayer. There was a harmony in their requests. They were united in their desire, but what were they praying for? (Acts 1:14)

I believe the only thing they could pray for was the last thing that Jesus spoke to them about. They knew that it was the will of the Father to give the Holy Spirit. Jesus had told them! They knew that they would become witnesses not through their own strength, but through the anointing of the Holy Spirit.

The promise, or the will of God, and the prayers of the saints poised them to be ready to receive all that God had promised them. They received the promise on the day of Pentecost. They did not panic in the waiting. They partnered with the Father. They were ready when God moved heaven on earth. Jesus had told them that when He went to the Father, the Father would send another helper, just like Him, the Holy Spirit. (John 14:15-18)

For the outside world looking at the disciples of Christ, they probably thought it was all over for them. The crucifixion had marked their demise. When Jesus spoke to them to "wait for the promised", His prophetic word reflected the will of God the Father and changed their vision or outlook.

Then, in a moment, when all of the waiting had been done and their prayers had ascended to heaven, heaven responded! At just the right time, in the middle of the feast of Pentecost, the atmosphere in the room was dramatically changed. There was a sound from heaven and a mighty rushing wind that filled the place in which they were assemble together. As promised, the Holy Spirit was given and the church was born. I think this perfectly demonstrates the Lord's Prayer: "Let your will be done on earth as it is in heaven."

Praying with the End in Sight

To know the will of God is such a powerful position in prayer. To understand the heart of the Father is to know the end at the beginning. When we get God's mind on a matter, it transforms every situation. The challenges we face that would normally cause us to meltdown in anxiety and fear are changed into places of comfort and peace. We see the same challenges from a kingdom perspective. Once God speaks into a situation, His word creates a place of supernatural faith.

To be able to grab hold of His word and know the promises of God is vital. They become a rock in our lives. The storms will rage and the obstacles will come but we can stand fast in the knowledge that God will do what He has promised. When we take hold of His word, we know we will come through the valley of the shadow of death. Every dry bone will live and the obstacles we face will surrender to the will of God.

Our eyes are not fixed on the waves that surround us, but on Jesus who meets us in the midst of the storm. Even when we feel like we are drowning, He reaches out His hand and lifts us up to where He is. With Jesus by our side, we can face every situation with confidence. The storm that was tormenting us becomes still. Just like Peter, we find ourselves on a supernatural journey. We are not drowning, but walking on water with Jesus and being led back to safety.

God loves to give us a glimpse into the future. He delights in sharing promises with us. When he speaks, He creates dreams in our hearts that take us beyond our wildest thoughts and imaginations. He paints a vibrant picture that's comforting to our soul. His promises encourage us in our journey and edify the spirit within us. It changes our focus from where we are to where we are going. We see beyond the objections of our mind to the countless possibilities that only our spirit man can catch. In a moment, our spirit man, who has been a slave to our mind, rises up. Our mind becomes subject to our spirit man which is communicating with God. As the scripture says, "We are renewed in the spirit of our mind." (Ephesians 3:23)

There is a light in the midst of the darkness. Hope is restored and our prayers are transformed.

How many times have Amanda and I have prayed for our children? They, like us, have gone through many struggles. Like all children, they have made decisions that we would not make. They have chosen to do things that we would not want them to do. And, like all parents, we have been brought to our knees in prayer.

We have stood in the gap and have gone through many levels of warfare on their behalf. We have called on God to rescue them and help them. We have cried, and at times, faced the fear that comes with some of the decisions they have made. Then, in the midst of the trials, God has rescued us from our own fears and imaginations. He has lifted our eyes and helped us see the same situation from a heavenly perspective. By revealing to us His will and reminding us of His promises for their lives, our prayers are transformed.

We stop praying out of panic and start declaring out of faith. We proclaim the promises. We pray all that God has said about them and we trust that He will do what He has said He will do.

Let's remember that when we pray the Lord's Prayer, we are praying "Let Your will be done on earth as it is in heaven." We are praying that heaven will invade earth; that His kingdom will invade our castles. Doesn't it make sense to get heaven's perspective? We should pray from the position that we are seated in, with Christ Jesus in the heavenly place. When we pray, we call down heaven's purposes upon earth and that includes our children.

Unfortunately, most people pray from an earthly, fallen perspective. We allow what's going on in the lives of our children to affect our thinking and the promises that God has made. Instead of praying from our position, seated with Christ in heavenly places, we pray from our fallen state of mind. We allow earth to affect heaven instead of releasing heaven on earth.

This can all change by asking the Father a simple question. What is His will or promise in the midst of the things your children are facing? Look at it through the eyes of Jesus. Adjust your stance. Position yourself with heaven on your side and pray with confidence in the will of the Father.

Obviously, understanding the will of the Father not only impacts our children, but our whole family, business, marriage, ministry, and church life. In every area of life there will be challenges. The enemy comes to kill, steal, and destroy. He will do all he can to stop you from fulfilling the call of God in your life.

There will be times when you face things that seem impossible. Situations will challenge all you stand for or are dreaming of, even dreams that have started in the heart of the Father and created vision in your lives. The very obstacles you face seem to steal the dreams God has placed in your heart. However, in the midst of those obstacles, we know the end even at the beginning. We don't pray out of fear by what we see in the natural, but out of faith and that which we know God has promised. We pray the promises of God!

If you have been going through a trial for what seem like forever or a difficult season that seems never ending, don't panic. All is not lost. Let's remember that Jesus is the author and finisher of our faith. He is the Alpha and Omega, the beginning and the end. He knows what He has started in you and what He will complete through you. The Bible declares that "He who has begun a good work in you is faithful to complete it." If it is not yet complete, it's because He has not yet finished with the thing He has promised you.

Hold fast to the promises and the will of God. His will creates unprecedented confidence through which we pray. Our prayers release those promises here or as Jesus said, "Heaven on earth."

Knowing the Will of God

Answering the question of how to know the will of God is a book in itself. In each of these areas I will share with you is just a glimpse into a greater adventure with God. I encourage you to seek God and go on a journey with Him to better understand His will.

The first area that reveals the will and nature of God is the Bible. This is such a great gift that God has given us. For many years, the Bible was hidden and taken from the common man. Our only access was through what others told us. We were told that only the priest knew what the Word of God said. All we could do was trust their words, but unfortunately, much of what they said was not even in the Bible.

Today, the Word of God (the Bible) is easily accessible and yet many, even believers, take little time to read it. It is full of the answers we need. It reveals the very heart of the Father. If we read it for ourselves, we would be amazed at what we would discover.

Many people have a picture of God that is not biblically accurate. They think that He is harsh and quick to judge, waiting to punish every little mistake we make. This affects the way we pray and as I wrote earlier, we approach God the Father as slaves and not sons and daughters. We approach in fear and not faith.

When you read the Bible for yourself you will discover that God the Father has already judged sin and paid the price for your mistakes. He gave His son, Jesus, to die on the cross so your sins would be forgiven, even removed! Now you as believers can come boldly to the throne of grace and converse with the Father. His mercies are new every morning. His love transforms every fear we have. The miracles we read of give us faith that there is nothing impossible for God. As we read of the many characters in the Bible, we see their mistakes and weaknesses, but God, in His grace, continues to rescue them and fulfill His promises.

As we read the Word of God, the lights are turned on. In areas where we had no direction, we use the Bible as a signpost pointing us in the way we should go. As we journey through life, it is like walking on paths that go through a forest. They twist and turn and at times they seem to disappear. The paths seem to be hidden, but suddenly a ray of light shines through the trees and we quickly discover where we are and where we need to go. Our way has been illuminated and as described in the book of Psalms, the Word is a light to our path.

We see our world from a different perspective. His truth sets us free from every fear and lie of the enemy.

The Word is a rock upon which we can stand and a fortress in times of battle. It is a belt around our waist holding all things together. It is a sword within our hand that we can use as a weapon against the enemy. The Word is the shoes upon our feet. Every step we take is guided and led by the Word of God.

There are so many things that we can say about the Word of God and then there are times when it's easier to look at Jesus. He is the Word made flesh. All that is written in the pages of the book and all the things that speak about the will and nature of the Father are clearly seen in the Son. Every truth it declares is displayed in the Son. Jesus said in regards to the will of the Father that "He only did what He saw His Father do." So when we look at the life of Jesus, the Word, we see a perfect reflection of the will of the Father. Wow, what a reflection of the truth we hold!

In reading the Word, we understand the will of the Father for our lives and in the lives of those around us. We see what He has done in the past in signs, wonders, and miracles and we start to understand what's possible in the present.

The moments I love most while reading the Word of God are when what we read comes alive. We call it revelation, but simply put, it is when the words jump off the page and grab hold of our hearts. That which is written on the pages become the voice and promise within our spirit.

The apostle Paul described it this way:

> "So then faith comes by hearing and hearing by the word of God." (Romans 10:17)

While reading the Word, that which is written in the Bible known as the "logos" (the written Word of God) comes alive. In an area of our life that seems empty, we catch hold of something that is said or written. In a place where there was no faith, faith comes. It jumps off the pages and we grab hold of it. The very words come to us as the voice of the Father. It is like He is standing in the room and prophesying directly to us. The written word that we are reading comes alive and becomes the "rhema" word of God. This is the "now word" which is the present word, needed for that moment. It is the spoken word of God that changes our present outlook. It is while reading the Word of God that we start hearing the Word of God. We catch hold of it, we meditate on it, and allow it to absorb into our hearts. This Word brings a new understanding of the will of God and allows us to see His nature in action.

The second way of understanding the will of the Father is through the Holy Spirit who loves to talk with us. I love the Holy Spirit so much. He is part of our everyday lives. He is always with us, from the moment we wake to the time we sleep. Even when we sleep, there are times that He invades our hearts with dreams and visions. King

Solomon said in the Song of Solomon, "Even though I sleep, my heart is awake. It is the voice of my beloved."

The Holy Spirit is a gift from the Father to His sons and daughters. He comes with a promise that we will not be left alone as orphans. At times, He is the voice of direction and other times, conviction. There are moments when He speaks and it sounds loud and clear. Then, at other times, He is the "still small voice." It is the whisper just beyond our own thinking or imagination. It is a thought that catapults us into hope. It is a sudden knowing that steadies our heart.

He is the great teacher; always pointing us to the life of Jesus and revealing the heart of the Father. He reminds us of things that God has said in the past; the very promises of God that help us in the present. He takes us by the hand and leads us into the will of the Father.

I love to talk to the Holy Spirit about the things that seem like a mystery and the things I don't understand. He opens my eyes so I can see the mystery from a different perspective. That which was hidden from me becomes visible and it's no longer a mystery.

How often have I come to realize that I have tried to understand my present life and circumstances with a natural mind? That's why they are a mystery. This is why I'm confused. I have failed to have a kingdom perspective. I need to know God's will and one of the ways the will of the Father is revealed is through the Holy Spirit:

> *"For what man knows the things of a man except the spirit of the man which is in him. Even so no one knows the things of God except the Spirit of God. Now we have received not the spirit of this world; but the Spirit who is from God, that we might know the things that have been freely given to us by God. These things we also speak, not in words which man's*

wisdom teaches, comparing spiritual things with spiritual. But the natural man does not receive the things of the Spirit of God, for they are foolishness to him; nor can he know them because they are spiritually discerned." (1 Corinthians 2:12-14)

This makes me jump up and down with joy because we have the Spirit of God so we can know the mind and heart of God! We can understand His will. That which is a mystery to others is a revelation to us. I hunger to know Him more.

This leads me to the prayer that the apostle Paul prayed, so it must be good!

"That the God of our Lord Jesus Christ, the Father of glory, may give to you the spirit of wisdom and revelation in the knowledge of Him, the eyes of your understanding being enlightened; that you my know what is the hope of His calling, what are the riches of the glory of his inheritance in the saints." (Ephesians 1:17-18)

How often I have prayed in times of struggle for the Holy Spirit, the Spirit of revelation, to reveal His will and perspective? In that moment, as my heart is enlightened, my understanding is changed and I start to see. I can then realign my prayers with the will of the Father. My confidence soars like the eagle because my perspective has changed. God is in control and I know again that "the effective, fervent prayers of a righteous man avails much." (James 5:16)

The third and final area that helps us understand the will of the Father is the prophetic ministry. This, for me, is a beautiful combination of the first two. It is a gift of the Spirit (as well as an office given by Christ) and never strays beyond the truth of the Word.

There are times when we become lost for words and our vision is dimmed. Then that someone, that believer who has heard God on our behalf, reveals His will. The words they share connect with our spirit. They confirm what we know is true. It puts the pieces of the puzzle together. Our outlook is changed. We are elevated from the valley to the mountaintop. We see the horizon and the way forward has been made clear.

This is seen when King Jehoshaphat and the children of God came under attack. The king was afraid and his fear drove him into the presence of God. He wanted to know what God was going to do. Would they be victorious or would they be defeated? Perhaps fear had clouded the king's vision? (2 Chronicles 20:3)

Out of the king's desperation, a feeling we have all felt at times, he calls everyone to prayer and fasting. In the midst of seeking God, God sends a prophet, a man called Jehaziel, with a word. With the prophetic word, Jehaziel calls the people to listen. Those who had been in a place of panic become still at the words of the prophet. The word is full of hope. There is a positive outcome. Their victory will be secured but they have to do something in the process. In learning the will of God, they have to believe it to be true. Their belief and trust in God will be seen in their actions. God always creates a place of action when He gives prophetic words.

The children of God were told not to fight and wrestle like the world. This battle would not be won through human strength. The children of Israel were called by the prophet to position themselves, to stand still. They were not to be moved with every imagination and thought. They were not to be double minded. They were to stand and see God in action.

The second thing they were told to do was sing. They were called to worship. Their eyes were set on God and not on the enemy. They were not to see the strength of the army that approached them, but they were to gaze on the salvation power of God. As they adjusted their vision and did their part, which was to sing, so they did the will of God for their lives. This changed everything. In that moment, as God was glorified, so heaven met earth. Their prayers were answered and God ambushed and overcame the enemy.

The prophetic ministry creates an agenda for prayer. It reveals what God is doing and what we need to do. It establishes us in His purpose and His will for our lives. With boldness we can say, "Let your kingdom come, let your will be done on earth as it is in heaven."

Chapter 5: On Earth As It Is In Heaven

Your kingdom come. Your will be done. <u>*On earth as it is in heaven.*</u>
(Matthew 6:10)

This is the picture of the perfection of heaven invading an imperfect world. It is prayer of hope that invites the God of heaven into the mess we have created on earth. It is a world that has been in chaos since the fall of man and a place where at times, we have all felt broken, lost, and helpless. Yet, in the midst of our confusion, we call out to God and invite heaven on earth. With a prayer, we respond to the one who has been knocking on the door of our hearts. As we let Jesus into our lives, so comes the kingdom of God and the hope of heaven touches earth.

How many times do we see this in the New Testament? Jesus, who was a love gift from the Father in heaven, sent to us, His creation. Jesus came not to fulfill His own will or to establish His own ministry, but that of the Father. Jesus preached the gospel of the kingdom. He demonstrated the rule and reign of God. This was a gospel not just of words, but of power. As He preached, so the power of heaven touched earth and the sick were healed, the demonized were set free, and the lost were saved.

When the kingdom of God comes on earth as it is in heaven, lives are miraculously transformed and changed. The impossible is made possible. Order comes in our chaos and hope is restored.

Let's see Jesus at work in the scriptures:

> Then Jesus went about all the cities and villages, teaching in their synagogues, preaching the gospel of the kingdom, and healing every sickness and every disease among the people. But when He saw the multitudes, He was moved with compassion for them, because they were weary and scattered like sheep having no shepherd. Then He said to His disciples the harvest is plentiful, but the laborers are few. Therefore pray the Lord of the harvest to send out laborers into the harvest. (Matthew 9:35-38)

> And when He had called His twelve disciples to Him, He gave them power over unclean spirits, to cast them out, and to heal all kinds of sickness and all kinds of disease. (Matthew 10:1)

> These twelve Jesus sent out……….. (Matthew 10:5)

(Please note that in the original text there was no chapter verse break between Matthew 9 and Matthew 10)

Jesus is doing His thing, preaching the gospel of the kingdom and demonstrating the gospel of the kingdom. He is bringing hope to the hopeless and restoring lives.

While ministering to the sick, Jesus is overwhelmed with compassion for the people. I believe this is supernatural compassion. This is where our spirit man is moved by the Spirit of God with the heart of the Father for the lost. It sees beyond the ugliness of man's rejection of God to the heart of man that is in desperate need of a shepherd or The Shepherd, Jesus.

As Jesus realizes the need, He also sees His weakness. As one man, He can only be in one place at a time and the need was great. More laborers are needed to carry out and demonstrate the gospel of the kingdom.

What Jesus does in the next moment is genius! He calls His disciples to pray. He takes a pressing need on earth and asks the disciples to present it to the Father in heaven. They were to pray to the Lord of the harvest and present the need. Jesus knew that there was a solution. I suspect He also knew what the solution was, but He wanted the disciples to feel the same compassion that He was moved with. He knew that if they caught the heart of the Father in heaven, they would be willing to do the mission on earth!

Up until this point, the disciples had watched and observed their teacher, Jesus, at work. They had seen what He had done. I am sure it created great excitement. Now they stand at a new junction in life. They had prayed and heaven was about to come to earth in a new way.

Jesus called the disciples to Him knowing they had prayed and had been prepared before the Father. It was here that they received the power of the Holy Spirit to go and do what Jesus had been doing. It was about to get real and their mission on earth was about to begin. With specific instruction, the disciples were sent.

As they were sent on their mission, we can see that their prayer to the Lord of the harvest had been answered. They became the very laborers that they had been praying for. How often have we been moved to pray for someone or something? Maybe we have felt compelled to pray for a particular people, group, or nation. As we are praying, we catch the heart of God for the very thing we are praying for. Like the disciples, this starts a new adventure for us. We become part of the solution to the problem. God invades our lives with heavenly desire and power. He then sends us with the power of the Holy Spirit to release the kingdom of heaven to others.

When we are praying for the kingdom to come on earth as it is in heaven, we are placing ourselves on a call to duty. This can be as simple as praying for a sick relative in the hospital. As we pray, we catch God's heart. We are moved with compassion for them. With love and boldness, we step out of our comfort zone and go on a kingdom mission. In ministering to our sick relative, heaven is released on earth in their lives.

Transferring Power and Authority

"On earth as in heaven" is about releasing or transferring that which is in the heart and mind of the Father here on earth. Let's see how the apostle Paul talks about this process:

> *Blessed be the God and Father of our Lord Jesus Christ, who has blessed us with every spiritual blessing in heavenly places in Christ. (Ephesians 1:3)*

The storehouse of heaven is full with every spiritual blessing we could ever need. It is not lacking in anything. To say that it is full and overflowing is a major understatement. It cannot run out of supply or options. Every blessing is at the Father's disposal and is given to us through Christ.

Jesus made a way through the cross and the shedding of His blood to come boldly to the Father who is in heaven. (Hebrews 10:19) He encourages us to pray, to seek, and to ask. Jesus said, "Whatever you ask in my name, believe and you will receive." All of these spiritual blessings in heavenly places are ours in Christ. Of course, we have to balance our requests with the will of the Father and a kingdom desire.

Paul tells us that there is a storehouse in heaven and it's accessible to us through Christ. The scripture goes on to tell us that Christ who "descended also ascended above all the heavens." (Ephesians 3:10) "He is now seated in heavenly places far above all principality and power, and might and every name that is named." (Ephesians 1:20-21) This is a position of rule and reign. It's a place of authority and power demonstrated by the fact that all things have been put under His feet. (Ephesians 1:22) This is a beautiful picture of Christ our King who with dominion, authority, and the keys of death rules over the earth.

Jesus is risen and is now at the "right hand of the Father," (Acts 2:33) praying and "making intercession for us." (Romans 8:34) I don't believe He is just praying to the Father, but with the Father. As they are one, they pray and move in synergy with the Holy Spirit for us, the church, and a world that is in need of salvation. They desire for heaven to come on earth.

This next part blows my mind because we, the church, are invited and positioned in heavenly places with Christ. It is a place of authority and power. We have to read the scripture to believe it:

> But God, who is rich in mercy, because of His great love with which He loved us, even when we were dead in trespasses, made us alive together with Christ (by grace you have been saved) and raised us up together, and made us sit together, in heavenly places in Christ Jesus. (Ephesians 2:4-6)

Wow! Unlike Christ, I know that we are not physically in heaven at this time. But we, in our salvation through Christ, have been raised together with Christ and we now sit with Him. What does this mean?

As Christ, who is the head of the body, (Ephesians 1:22-23) has been raised to sit in authority in heavenly places, so we sit in that same authority with Him. I believe that from this position we get to do what Christ is doing. If Jesus is praying at the right hand of the Father and we are seated with Him, then we, too, are to praying from heaven. Our feet may be on earth, but our authority is with our throne and position in heaven.

Stand back and see the picture. Paul tells us that the storehouse of heaven is full of spiritual blessings through Christ. It is through Christ that we have access to these spiritual blessings through prayer. We have been seated with Him and have the same authority. We can pray for a release of the kingdom on earth as it is in heaven. We are not praying selfish prayers because we are building the kingdom and not our castles. We are not praying our will, but His will, which we have come to understand through relationship.

When we understand the authority we have been given, it changes our outlook. We are not gazing at a thing, a problem, or challenge from the middle of a mess, but we have been elevated to see from a heavenly perspective. We have been given the seat of authority and the power or keys to unlock heaven on earth.

Jesus told Peter:

> "And I will give you the keys of the kingdom, and whatever you bind on earth will be bound in heaven, and whatever you loose on earth will be loosed in heaven." (Matthew 16:19)

The one who has the master key can give keys to those who work with Him. Only He who has authority can give authority. Jesus said after His resurrection, "All authority has been given to me in heaven (first) and (then) on earth." It was with this authority and with these keys that Jesus opened a whole new dimension of prayer to Peter and the church. (Matthew 28:18) Together with Christ, we are called to pray from a heavenly position. We are then positioned to proclaim and bring the kingdom on earth as the messengers of Christ, with the authority of Christ.

Apostle Paul's Prayer: Heaven on Earth

The apostle Paul was teaching the Ephesian church about prayer, in particular, spiritual warfare. He encouraging them to stand against all the works of the enemy and not just to stand, but to keep standing. He wanted them to know that they were in a battle, but they were also on the winning side. They had all the weapons they needed to overcome the enemy. Paul reminded them that this battle was not just a natural battle, but it was supernatural. It was not against flesh and blood, men and women, but the spirits that control them. This is a further aspect of the authority of the church that has been given as we are seated with Christ in heavenly places. (Ephesians 6:10-17)

As Paul was teaching them about spiritual warfare, he encouraged them to pray for him:

> *Praying always with all prayer and supplication in the Spirit, being watchful till the end with all perseverance for all the saints – and for me, that I may open my mouth boldly to make known the mystery of the gospel (of the Kingdom) for which I am an ambassador in chains, that I may speak boldly, as I ought to speak." (Ephesians 6:19)*

I think this is a most revealing portion of scripture in relation to prayer. Paul not only teaches about spiritual authority and our position in being seated with Christ, he also desired action with prayer. This reminds me of the scripture we shared earlier when Jesus called His disciples to pray. As they prayed to the Lord of the harvest, so they were sent into the harvest.

Here, Paul wanted the church to know its power. He was revealing to them the spiritual battle. He encouraged them to use their heavenly authority in the spirit realm against the unseen principals and powers. At the same time, he called them to pray that a door would be opened here on earth so he could preach the kingdom.

We are to pray with heavenly authority as we are seated with Christ. We are to impact both the seen and the unseen. The kingdom come impacts heaven and that impact is seen in the kingdom coming on earth.

Jesus Praying and Releasing Heaven on Earth

Jesus is our perfect model of prayer, especially when it comes to releasing heaven on earth. We read in Mark that Jesus has been up long before daylight, praying. Before His busy day started, He found a place to hang out with the Father. He needed His time in His Father's presence. He needed a solitary place before the business of the day.

> *Now in the morning, having risen a long while before daylight, He went out and departed to a solitary place; and there He prayed. And Simon and those who were with Him searched for Him. When they found Him, they said to Him, "everyone is looking for you." But He said to them, "Let us go into the next towns that I may preach there also, because for this purpose, I have come forth." And He was preaching in*

their synagogues throughout all Galilee and casting out demons. (Mark 1:35-40)

Jesus separates Himself from the disciples long before the day starts. Most people look to start the day with a mindset of "business as usual." It's just another day. Let's get to work! Jesus has a different approach. Every day is unique with a kingdom purpose. Every day has the potential of a supernatural impartation if we make ourselves available.

We know that Jesus was not looking to do His will, but the will of the Father. Jesus started the day in the presence of God to understand what the day would hold and what God would "will" for Him to do.

Suddenly, the disciples find Him. They exclaim, "everyone is looking for you!" It is almost funny how Jesus ignores their statement and declares what they are about to do. When I read this, I see Jesus in prayer or conversation with the Father. This is where He receives instruction for the next thing. In the following moment, He has been given direction and the mission is on. I believe that while He is in prayer, He gets a download or a divine strategy of what they must do next. Jesus discovers His purpose for that day or the season. He is energized and ready when the disciples come looking for Him. When they say "everyone is looking for you", He responds with, "Let's go!" In other words, they had a job to do and He was focused on the task at hand. Jesus then tells them where they are going with the statement, "We are going to the next town" to preach the gospel.

As soon as Jesus goes to the next town, the kingdom is released on earth. The gospel is preached and taught in the synagogue. The demonized are set free and if you read on, there is an incredible encounter with a man suffering with leprosy. Let's call this a divine meeting or encounter in which the man receives a miracle. I don't believe that the man was in the right place at the right time as much as I believe that Jesus was in the right place at the right time.

Jesus demonstrates "Your kingdom come, Your will be done, On earth as in heaven." By taking time to pray and seeking the will of God, He caught hold of a kingdom idea. Fresh from heaven, He knew His next move. That which He received in prayer and from heavenly places, Jesus released on earth.

The kingdom is more than that which we surrender to. It's more than the rule and reign of heaven. It is something we carry when we surrender and make ourselves available to God. It's in the moments that we catch a heavenly idea, revelation, or vision that the impossible is made possible. Miracles start to take place and lives are changed.

Hidden within this passage is another great lesson for leaders or anyone who finds themselves under the lens of popularity. The moment a leader gains recognition, popularity grows. With this natural growth comes a demand on your time. People come looking for you just like the disciples came looking for Jesus. Popularity tempts a person to perform; to meet the people's needs. The problem with this mentality is that we often find we are building our kingdom or castle and not God's kingdom.

I believe that Jesus knew how demand can cloud our vision. Jesus took the time to separate Himself and refocus in the presence of the Father in prayer. It is in His presence that He realigns His purpose. It is kingdom purpose that rightly positions us to be effective in bringing the kingdom of God on earth as it is in heaven.

Heavenly Blueprint

We see this style of prayer again at another important junction in the ministry of Jesus. Transition was taking place. The Old Testament with all its laws was being fulfilled and the final curtain was coming down. Jesus came with a new message: the gospel of the kingdom. It was refreshing, revolutionary, and challenged the status quo. What Jesus brought was like new wine. In His own words; old wineskins, old religion. Put another way, even the old covenant could not contain the new things God was doing.

The way that people came to God in worship, prayer, and sacrifice was changing. The place in which the glory of God would be seen and experienced was in renovation. The tabernacle had long gone and the importance of the temple was changing.

That which was made with bricks and mortar would give way to a new temple. This new temple would truly be a light to the world and contain the glory and power of God like no temple before it. This temple was not stuck in one place, but would be seen where people met to worship Jesus. It is a temple made with living stones; a spiritual house with a holy priesthood made up of believers in Christ. The sacrifices they brought would no longer be bulls, goats, or animal sacrifices. The new sacrifice would be known as "spiritual sacrifice," the prayers and worship of the saints. It was the giving of their hearts and a willingness to lay down their lives for another.

The foundation of the old ways, the old covenant, was made with the twelves tribes of Israel. This new temple of living stone would have a different foundation. It would not start with twelve tribes, but twelve apostles who caught and carried the message of the kingdom.

One of the things that I love about God is that He has a plan. He has a blueprint in heaven for what He wants to do on earth and He loves to share it with us. When Moses instructed Israel to build a tabernacle, it wasn't just a good idea. He didn't sit down with a paper and pen or a rock and a piece of flint. He didn't come up with a plan, he received the plan. God gave him a blueprint of what He wanted him to build.

> *...... who serve the copy and shadow of the heavenly things, as Moses was divinely instructed when he was about to make the tabernacle. For He said, "See that you make all things according to the pattern shown you on the mountain." (Hebrews 8:5)*

When we read the account in the Old Testament, we discover that Moses was called up into the mountain. It is here that he was covered by the cloud, a form of the Holy Spirit, and experienced the glory of God. This call was a call into a place of prayer and relationship with the Father. While on the mountain, Moses received detailed instructions for forty days. He learned about the role of the priesthood, the sacrifices, and how to build the tabernacle according to a heavenly blueprint. (Exodus 24:9-18.) This is truly a shadow and example of "Your kingdom come, Your will be done on earth as it is in heaven."

When I read this, I see that God loves to reveal divine strategies and instruction. If He did this in the Old Testament, why would He not do it in the New Testament which brings a better covenant with better promises?

Jesus knew that He needed His Father's insight and instruction. So, like Moses, He found a mountain and prayed all night.

Now it came to pass in those days that He went out to the mountain to pray, and continued all night to pray to God. And when it was day, He called His disciples to Himself and from them He chose twelve whom he also named apostles. (Luke 6:12-13)

Jesus continued to pray all night. There was an urgent matter at hand and He needed revelation. Again, we see that Jesus did not rely on his own insight, but He sought the will of the Father. In hearing from heaven in the place of prayer on the mountain, He received the blueprint. Just like Moses, Jesus knew how to build and lay the foundation of a new temple, a temple of living stones.

As soon as morning came, Jesus called the disciples to him and out of them he chose the twelve to represent the kingdom. He received heaven's blueprint and it had a direct impact on earth.

It is interesting that we read here that Jesus called the twelve whom He chose as apostles. Not only was God doing a new thing by raising up a new living temple, He was using new language. Never before had the word "apostle" been used to describe a person's gift or calling. It cannot be found in the Old Testament, but its meaning was powerful and was a further reflection of the kingdom the apostles were to bring.

The word "apostle" was not first a biblical word, but it was used in the Roman Empire. The disciples would have known and understood the term. The word "apostle" described those who were called and sent by the Roman Empire to another land. They were sent with specific instruction to establish the empire or kingdom of Rome in another land. They were to set up a colony of Rome. It would have Roman governors, laws, and taxes. If you went to one of these colonies, you would see a reflection of Rome.

Every time we read the Greek word for "apostle" in the New Testament, we read the word "apostolos." It carries the same thought and imagery as the word used by the Romans. The dominant meaning of the word is someone who is "sent" with authority and power to establish the kingdom.

Jesus, our apostle, (Hebrews 3:1) was "sent" by the Father in heaven to earth. He was commissioned to establish the kingdom of God. The rule and reign of heaven was to be released on earth. The effect was a release of the supernatural power of God. Lives were transformed and changed. The natural gave way to miracles.

Jesus, knowing His future and eventual sacrificial death, looked beyond the grave to the day of Pentecost upon which the church would be born. He knew that it would be the disciples' job and our responsibility to bring the kingdom of God here on earth. So with this in mind, after a night in prayer, He received heaven's instruction – the blueprint of heaven. Jesus called and commissioned the twelve as apostles, "sent ones", and they were to bring the kingdom of heaven on earth.

Again I pray, let "Your kingdom come, Your will be done, on earth as it is in heaven," would be more than just another prayer in your life. I pray that it would become a demonstration of the kingdom here on earth through your life.

Jesus and His Appendix to the Lord's Prayer

There is an aspect to the Lord's Prayer told by Luke that blows me away. I love Matthew's account, but there is an addition here that grabs hold of my heart. In Luke's account, we find Jesus praying and the disciples are watching. They wait for Him to finish and they are so moved by what they have witnessed that they want to know how to pray. You can almost sense the excitement in their voices as they cry out for Him to teach them to pray.

Like in the book of Matthew, Luke describes the Lord's Prayer. As we know, this is powerful, but it's what Jesus teaches next that captivates the desire of my heart to pray "on earth as it is in heaven."

Many people stop at the end of the Lord's Prayer and fail to read on. In reading further, we find the truths that Jesus spoke about as further illustrated in a parable and exhortation to the disciples. To begin, we see that there is no "amen" at the end of Luke's description of the Lord's Prayer. This is because he has not finished sharing what Jesus taught them. He had more to say on the matter. Just because the prayer had come to a close, it did not conclude all that Jesus had to say regarding this particular way of praying.

Jesus gives us the outline of the Lord's Prayer and then continues to teach on prayer by adding the need for persistence in prayer. He shares that if we were to find ourselves in an hour of need, we would seek a friend for help. We would not be concerned with the time of day or the inconvenience of our plea, just the urgency of the need. Even though the friend may seem reluctant at first to get out of bed and help, he will responds because of our persistence. He will be moved by our cry and therefore respond with kindness. Jesus was emphasizing the fact that our persistence can move a reluctant friend. This led to a greater truth. Jesus told them that if a persistent cry could move a friend, how much more could persistent prayer move the heart and hand of our heavenly Father to respond to His children? As we hold that thought, let's remember this illustration in light of the Lord's Prayer that starts with "Our Father!"

Jesus continues this theme:

> *"So, I say to you, ask, and it will be given to you; seek, and you will find; knock, and it will be opened to you. For everyone who asks receives, and he who seeks finds, and to him who knocks it will be opened. If a son asks for bread from any father among you, will he give him a stone? Or if he asks for a fish, will he give him a serpent instead of a fish? Or if he asks for an egg, will he offer him a scorpion? If you then being evil, know how to give good gifts to your children, how much more will your <u>heavenly Father give the Holy Spirit to those who ask Him!</u>" (Luke 11:9-13)*

Jesus already has the disciples' attention when He refers to asking for bread from a friend. They understand friendship. They shared their lives with each other and with their friends. I'm sure as they heard this, they thought of each other. They knew they could rely upon the other in a time of need. With this in mind, Jesus cleverly changes the teaching. He moves from friend to father. If a friend could do this, how much more could a father do, who should be closer than a friend? Now He has them where He wants them in their thinking. If an earthly father would give you bread, how much more would your heavenly Father give you as a gift from heaven? Again, let's remember that the Lord's Prayer invites "heaven on earth."

The context of this teaching is that we should be persistent in praying to our Father in heaven who is better than a friend. Our persistence should take us on a journey where we "ask, seek, and knock." This persistent prayer will result in God responding to us. We have a promise that we will "receive, find, and it will be opened to us." This is truly a picture of heaven being released on earth.

As soon as Jesus shares this truth of persistence, He quickly captures the attention of the disciples again. He shifts from using a "good friend" to the relationship between sons and fathers. Jesus illustrates the fact that any good father will respond to the need of their sons. The son is rightly positioned in the family and in his relationship to a father to ask for the things he needs. A good father will respond in kind. He will meet the request that has been made by his son by giving what has been asked of him. If he needs bread, that is what he will get. The father will not give something other than what has been asked.

Then, with a stroke of genius, Jesus links the Lord's Prayer, our relationship with our heavenly Father, and the release of heaven on earth. *".... If you then being evil, know how to give good gifts to your children, how much more will your heavenly Father give the Holy Spirit to those who ask Him?"*

In this statement, Jesus takes us beyond our need for bread and gifts and takes us to the gift of the Holy Spirit. For me, it is the ultimate gift given by the Father and releases "heaven on earth" like never before. The only way that Jesus was able to preach and demonstrate the kingdom of heaven was through the power of the Holy Spirit. It was the anointing upon Him that enabled Him to move in the miraculous. (Luke 4:18)

Jesus told the disciples that when He goes to the Father, the Father who is in heaven would send the Holy Spirit. (John 14:16) Again, after the resurrection of Jesus, He instructs the disciples to wait in Jerusalem for the promise of the Holy Spirit. He reminded them that when the Holy Spirit came upon them, He would give them power to be witnesses in Jerusalem, Judea, Samaria, and to the ends of the earth. In other words, they would receive heaven on earth. The Father would give them the gift of the Holy Spirit so they would be able to preach the gospel just like Jesus. The gospel is the kingdom of God which is both proclaimed and demonstrated with signs and wonders following.

If that was good for the disciples, it is good for us. All we need to do is come to our Father in heaven who is more faithful than a friend and more loving than our earthly father. Jesus gives us a promise that if we ask for the gift from heaven who is the Holy Spirit, the Father will give Him to us. In the same way that the disciples received the Holy Spirit on the day of Pentecost, so too can we can receive Him today in our living rooms and churches.

In the moment that we ask and receive the Holy Spirit, we are changed. God takes ordinary men and women and starts to do extraordinary things through our lives. Every promise, calling, or challenge that seemed impossible is now possible because of the anointing. The moment we receive, we are repositioned. Not only are we sons and daughters who have the right to ask, we become kings. The very same anointing that blessed King David and many other men and women of God has also blessed you. In the Old Testament it was only available for the few, but in the New Testament, it's for all believers in Christ. King David was anointed to rule and reign and establish the kingdom of Israel. We have been anointed to rule and reign and bring the kingdom of heaven on earth.

Jesus taught the Lord's Prayer by saying; "Our Father in heaven, hallowed be Your name. Your kingdom come, Your will be done on earth as in heaven." Jesus then illustrated this by encouraging the disciples to be persistent in asking, seeking, and knocking in pursuit of the Father in heaven. He is a Father who is better than a friend and more gracious in His gifts than an earthly father. He is a Father who desires to release heaven on earth. All it takes is for us to ask and when we ask, we will receive the Holy Spirit. It's the Holy Spirit that has been sent from the Father in heaven which enables us to bring the kingdom here on earth.

Chapter 6: Give Us This Day Our Daily Bread

"Give us this day our daily bread" (Matthew 6:11)

There is something beautiful about the faithfulness of God. He is a Father who always looks out for His children. He already knows our needs before we ask. He has the answer; He is the answer.

Faithfulness is only one side of the coin and the other side is trust. When God displays His faithfulness, it creates something in us. It calls us to another level of relationship. This is the place of greater trust. Faithfulness and trust are developed over a period of time. It is shown and experienced on a daily basis. It is the foundation of any good relationship. The heart of the Father is that we develop our prayer life which demonstrates our trust in God's faithfulness.

God's faithfulness is more than just giving us what we want or need for the day. It's the consistency of being there for us and meeting our needs on a daily basis. Those needs may be natural, material, or spiritual.

It is interesting that there has been much debate over this portion of the Lord's Prayer. Was Jesus encouraging the disciples to pray for natural bread or spiritual bread? Depending on the commentary you read or who you listen to, you will get a different answer.

I have been led by the Holy Spirit to use this scripture to pray for both my natural and spiritual needs. I don't think it has to be one or the other, but can be both. The greater truth is that I trust the Father with all of my needs on a daily basis. The Father is faithful to show up and meet with me, answering my spiritual needs as well as meeting my natural needs. So, as we continue to examine this part of the Lord's Prayer, we will look at both our natural and spiritual daily needs.

Your Turn

As we press into this area of the Lord's Prayer, there is a gentle but purposeful shift. We started by praying, "Your kingdom come, Your will be done, on earth as in heaven." Then we shift to "give us this day our daily bread." The focus changes from us praying for others, (or becoming the vessel through which the kingdom comes to others) to praying for ourselves.

This is amazing, kingdom thinking. It is more natural for us when praying to first pray for our own needs before we pray for others. We often have a list of things we want or need God to answer. By praying for others first, it changes our focus. It removes the selfish part of our prayer life, which we all have. As we become sacrificial in putting others first and praying for them, we are rightly positioned to pray for ourselves. The victim mentality in us that wants to shout "why me" or "help me," becomes a vessel for God to use me. It is not that our needs are less important than theirs, it just puts them into a better perspective. Our needs become less exaggerated and more focused in light of the greater prayer of inviting the kingdom to come and God's will to be done.

Not only does it change the way we see our needs, it changes the atmosphere in which we pray. It is often easier to have faith while praying for others. We know what God can and will do for them. As we pray for others, confidence grows in us and lays a foundation of faith for us. Now we are ready to pray for our own needs from a position of faith which has been established in the will of God.

Jesus demonstrates this kingdom type of thinking. We read earlier about the time that Jesus instructed His disciples to pray for laborers. Then, those who prayed became the laborers that Jesus called to the mission field. He gave them power and sent them to the lost sheep of Israel. They were commissioned to preach the gospel of the kingdom with signs and wonders following. They were sent with instruction to heal the sick, cast out demons, and even raise the dead. They had prayed and Jesus had prayed for them by calling them to Himself and giving them power. Now they were sent to bring the kingdom to others. (Matthew 9:37 – Matthew 10:8)

As they were being sent, Jesus told them that they were not to be worried about their daily needs. It is almost a throwaway comment unless you catch it. "Go preach and demonstrate the kingdom, and by the way, don't worry about stuff. You will be taken care of." They didn't need money, overnight bags, or food. They just needed to go and do the will of God. As they were faithful to go and put others first and bring the kingdom, so they would receive their daily needs. They had to trust and as we know, God is always faithful.

As the disciples were encouraged by Jesus, so are we. We are told to "seek first the kingdom of God and His righteousness and all these things will be added to us." We can rest assured that when we do the will of the Father by seeking first the kingdom, God will give us our daily needs.

God has given us His word. He has promised that He will turn up and meet our needs.

Give Us….

How many times have we woken in the morning with a pressing need? We have a challenge in front of us that just won't go away. We have even wondered at times if we will get through the day because the burden seems so heavy. We have packed the kids' lunch, sent them to school, worshipped, prayed for others, and still our needs are staring us in the face.

The problem is that we have a pressing need. As long as we hold on to it, it is our problem that only we can solve. The moment we realize that we do not have the answer or resources, we either collapse under the weight of it or surrender it to God. If we choose to surrender it, the problem is transferred into the hands of God. He never looks at a thing as a problem because He has infinite answers and solutions. Our problems are a place where God the Father demonstrates His power!

We cry out or pray out "give us" because we don't have what we need. At the same time, we know that God is more than able to supply all of our needs. We call out to the one who holds the answer. Our breakthrough is safely in the hands of God. In the moment we cry out, we display both desperation in our situation and faith in God, who we trust will answer us. Those two things don't seem to fit together. Desperation and faith are like oil and water.

God is not looking for the religious version of you who says the right thing at the right time. He is looking for the authentic you. He doesn't want you to pretend that everything is okay while you are struggling inside. He wants you to be real with where you are at in the moment and real in your request.

We see an example of this as we read the gospel account of a man who has a sick child. His boy is epileptic and he needs a miracle. The father comes to the disciples and asks them to pray. He demonstrates his faith by bringing the boy to them. Instead of the boy getting better after prayer, he gets worse. We have all been there. In times when we hoped things would get better, they sometimes get worse. These times challenge our faith, but we have to hold on. Don't quit. Press on because God will be faithful to His promises.

The father of the boy could have quit and given up, but instead he came to Jesus. He sought out the one who had the answer. When he came to Jesus, he explained to Him what had happened and that his boy was still sick. Jesus said for him to just believe and the impossible will become possible. We would not be wrong in thinking he hadn't already tried this. He had believed, he had brought the child to the disciples, but Jesus was looking for something more. He wanted the man to be real. He didn't want to know what he had already done, but where he was at in that moment of need.

Jesus wanted to dig below the surface of the need to what was happening in the heart of the man. In times of need, we can all put on a fake smile or portray a false reality. On one hand, we have to hold on to the promises of God. This is faith in the unseen. At the same time, Jesus is asking us how we are coping or dealing with the matter at hand. Where are we spiritually and what's going on in our hearts? Jesus always deals with the issues of the heart.

The man responds with tears in his eyes, "Lord, I believe; help my unbelief." Just like the "give us" prayer, there is a realization that we cannot do any more. The man was real in his request and sincere in his feelings. Jesus responds to the authentic, real cry of the man. He rebuked the demon in the boy and he was made whole. (Mark 9:23-25)

"Give us" brings us to a place that makes us realize that we have run out of options. We have done all we can. We have told others about the problem and nothing has changed. Our family and friends do not have the answers or the resources we need. We are left with one thing to do and that is "give!" The moment we give Him our prayer, our giving up becomes a "give us." Our surrender becomes the place in which we experience the supernatural presence and power of God. We have opened the door and sent the invitation to the Father who has been waiting for an opportunity to move.

We should not be afraid of the challenges before us as the answer or response to our cry is safely in the hands of God. We are often paralyzed when staring at the size of our need. The Bible tells us that all we need is a mustard seed amount of faith. The smallest amount of faith will move a mountain or the greatest problem that is in front of us. The size of the mountain doesn't change the amount of faith that is required. When God looks at the mountains before you, whether great or small, they are just the same. From heaven's perspective they are all just hills or bumps on the horizon.

We are mistaken in thinking that a greater need requires God to move in a greater way. The law of the supernatural is the same regardless of the size of the problem. God spoke a word to create a father of many nations through Abraham and to create the heavens and the earth. One might look bigger than the other, but to God, they required the same thing. He spoke a word and it was created, it was done!

For me, there is no question that God is able to do all that He has promised. He will show up and meet your need. You just have to "give up" your prayer and watch the Father "give us our daily bread."

> *And my God shall supply all your needs according to His riches in glory by Christ Jesus. (Philippians 4:19)*

> *Blessed be the God and Father of our Lord Jesus Christ, who has blessed us with every spiritual blessing in heavenly places in Christ. (Ephesians 1:3)*

This is Your Day

Every day is the day of the Lord. It is a day in which He loves to move and reveal His love to us. He is in complete control. Nothing takes Him by surprise. This is also your day to receive from the presence and hand of God.

> *This is the day the Lord has made; We will rejoice and be glad in it. (Psalm 118:24)*

No matter what you feel when you get out of bed today or what challenges you face, there is a reason to be glad. No matter how much the struggles and storms of life want to steal your peace and strength, there is a reason to rejoice. Let your sorrow be turned into joy as laughter fills your being and your words reflect the promises of heaven. This is your day; a day that God is in control.

This is the day the Lord has made. There is something supernatural about this day. God made it and He intends to make Himself known in it. The Hebrew word for "made" is a word that is used repeatedly in the book of Genesis. It is used when God made the firmament and when he made two great lights, the sun and the moon. It is the same word in Genesis which declares when God the Father, Son, and Holy Spirit decided to create something unique. In agreement they said "Let us make man in Our image."

Time and again we see this powerful word. It affirms that what God creates is not wasted on this day. It's a word that makes something out of nothing. It is repeated 2638 times throughout the Old Testament revealing the wonders of God. It speaks of the unending resources and creativity of God. It is used to describe His presence in this day, your day - a day "the Lord has made."

God has made this day and He intends to move and create for you something out of nothing. All possibilities may seem to have gone or they may be beyond your reach, but God has created this day and He will move in it.

The truth I want you to catch as you approach the Father in prayer is that He is a present Father. He is not just the God of yesterday or tomorrow, but He is present today.

> *God is our refuge and strength, a very present help in trouble. (Psalm 46:1)*

How many children have had so-called relationships with their earthly father who is there, but not present? This can be a challenge for all of us. The distractions of life take our attention and those who need it the most don't receive it. They cry out but are not always heard. Or, how many have had fathers that turn up when they feel like it? They may even forget important dates or events. They are fathers who go missing.

We often relate to our heavenly Father through the eyes of children with absent parents. We have no real expectation to be heard even though we cry out. We have no real trust that He will turn up. Thankfully, our Father in heaven has not been made after the image of men, but he is the perfect Father who always hears and always responds. He is a very present help in times of trouble.

Let me clarify what I mean by "trouble". This is not just the stuff that troubles us, but also the troubles that we have created by our own decisions and choices in life. In both areas, we just need to call out. He is faithful to answer. Our unfaithfulness cannot change His faithfulness. The love of God casts out all fear; all fear of abandonment, rejection, or the lies telling us that we will not be heard. This is a lie the enemy often reinforces by causing us to focus on natural relationships in which we have been let down. Our heavenly Father is different. As we call out to Him, He answers and proves that He is a present and faithful Father. As we lean into Him, we will feel His embrace and receive answers to our prayers.

Today we can choose to place our day into the hands of God. Our day will then take on a new reality as we discover what God intended the day to be. Our day becomes the day the Lord has made.

When I think about how present God is, I always think about how He revealed himself to Moses. When Moses asked God His name, He told him that He was "I Am who I Am." He revealed Himself as the self-existing, eternal God that lives outside of time. At the same moment, God revealed himself as present. He stepped into Moses' time as the "I Am", a present God ready to deliver the children of Israel out of slavery.

In the book of Hebrews Chapter 11, we read about men and women of faith. It describes them as those who trusted God. It then

Lord, help our attention to bear fruit not death

Dec 29/2018

encourages us as present day believers to have the same faith in God. We are to approach God with faith, believing that He will move heaven and earth on our behalf. In other words, He will release heaven on earth.

The writer of Hebrews encourages believers to come to God believing that "He is". As such, "He is" the rewarder of those who diligently seek Him. (Hebrews 11:6) Again, the words "He is" point to the fact that God is the eternal, all existing one and at the same time He is the answer. He is a very present help in times of trouble. There is no truth, revelation, or resource that is beyond Him. In fact, all truth, revelation, and answer is in Christ Jesus.

This revelation is not just that He was or He will be, but "He is" the present one. He transcends times and days. His presence is not restricted to our yesterday or our tomorrow. "He is" present today to respond to our daily prayers.

Our Daily Bread

Not only will God turn up today, He will turn up daily. He is ever present. Just because we received something miraculous from God yesterday doesn't mean He won't show up again today. We have not used up all of our wishes. This is not a movie in which we get a limited number of requests like the genie in the lamp. In fact, the opposite is true. God showed Himself faithful yesterday and this becomes a foundation stone for what we can believe of God today. Also, whatever God did yesterday or today is a testimony in our lives. Every "testimony of Jesus is a spirit of prophecy." (Revelation 19:10) Every breakthrough and answer in prayer creates a picture in our lives. It is evidence of what God has done and foreshadows what He will continue to do in our lives.

When I think about this in my own life, I have discovered that the things God did yesterday in my life act as a seed. They are just the beginning of what he wants to do. If I needed to trust God for $100, it is a foundation for trusting God for $1,000 in the future.

One of the things I love about how God moved in the past is the fact that it becomes a weapon of faith in the present. It creates an expectation that God can and will do it again. The problem comes when we limit God to what He did yesterday or we expect Him to move in the same way today. This is a new day. We cannot say how God will move or what He will do, but we can be confident that He will answer our daily prayer.

God's desire to reveal Himself and meet our daily needs is seen in how He interacts with the children of Israel. After Moses led the children of Israel out of bondage and captivity, they find themselves in a desert or wilderness. There are not enough natural resources to support this great number of people. At this point, they need more than a meal. They need a miracle of lifestyle. They don't need a once in a lifetime experience, they need a daily encounter. (Exodus 16)

God hears their cry and answers their prayer. In fact, their cry was not so much a prayer but was more of a complaint. They felt stuck in the middle of a wilderness and they thought they were going to die. Even though they complained, God, in His mercy, answered them in a beautiful way.

God told them that He would "rain bread from heaven." Every day they would have fresh bread and they were to gather just enough for the day. Then, on the sixth day, they were to gather a double portion, twice as much. This is so they would have enough for this day and for the next which was the sabbath or the day of rest.

This is truly a heaven on earth moment of God responding to the needs of the people. The children of Israel received their daily bread. This would continue all the days they were in the wilderness. While they had no ability to farm the land, they would receive from the hand of God. The moment they stepped into their promised land, the manna or bread from heaven ceased. They no longer needed this daily miracle because God had given them a miracle land in which they could harvest.

The greater truth about manna from heaven or receiving daily bread has little to do with what we receive. What we need is beyond our resources, but God has a plan and is able to supply all that we need and much more. The lesson He wants us to learn is about trust and faithfulness.

Unless we trust a person, we will not put faith in them. We may have a need but they have not proved trustworthy in our lives. However, as we grow in relationship with people, we come to understand if they are trustworthy. We learn from experience whether or not they will do what they say they will do. We discover if they will show up or go missing in times of need.

The lesson that God wanted to teach the children of Israel was that He is a faithful God. He knew the need and He would meet the need every day. It was more than a one-off thing. He was and is trustworthy. Even though they rebelled and did not believe God would help them to enter the promised land, God did not change His heart or nature in providing for His children.

The more we experience God's faithfulness, the more we trust and have faith. We may begin the journey by asking and receiving bread from heaven on the first day. It then takes a step of faith to only gather what we need, trusting that God will bring more the next day.

As we use what God has given us, we wake the next morning in anticipation, but maybe also wondering. Will we receive fresh bread from heaven today like we did yesterday? As we arise, we discover that God has been faithful again and again and again. He is our daily bread!

Our ability to believe in the faithfulness of God is developed through a relationship of trust and provision. There are times when God will only give us enough for the day even though He can give us enough for the next year. He wants us to use what He has given us so He can then give us more. If we hold onto it and don't use what He has given us, we display a lack of faith. We are scared that we will run out of bread. This is a poverty mentality. We have to come to learn to trust God for our daily bread. We can rest assured that if we use what we have for that day, God will move again tomorrow and soon we will develop a daily miracles lifestyle.

A process then develops in which He instructs us to steward what He has given us. Just like Israel, we need to take that which is required for the day and the next day. That which we have is not just for the day, but for the next two days or for the next season. How can we know when it is for the day or for the next two days? The answer lies in our relationship with Him. We are called to stay in close communication, receiving and seeking how we should use what He has given. I believe God will make clear when we are to trust for daily provision and when we are to steward what He has given us for a season.

God has revealed His nature as one who is faithful. This is to create trust in us; a trust that removes anxiety and fear. It is a trust that is not moved by circumstances or challenges but sees beyond the things we have in the natural. This trust creates faith in a God who hears our prayers and miraculously rains down bread from heaven, providing our daily bread.

Natural Bread

I love how Jesus looks at life and all its challenges. The need for daily bread, food, and provision are not a concern, but a place of trust. Hunger is not to be feared as we have an expectation in God that He will meet our hunger and we will be filled. God has already predetermined to bless you. Your daily bread is waiting for you. (Matthew 5:6) That area which feels empty will be filled to the place where nothing is lacking or in need. God will not leave us hungry. King David declared:

> *"I have been young, and now am old; yet and I have never seen the righteous forsaken. Nor his descendants begging bread." (Psalm 37:25)*

God will be faithful to us in our hour of need. He is at hand, ready and waiting for you on a daily basis to trust and pray. Your prayer is a key that unlocks heaven on earth. God is waiting to respond, you just need to ask. The Bible say "we have not because we ask not." It is time to ask.

As I said at the beginning of this chapter, our prayer for "daily bread" can be for natural or spiritual bread. Here we are going to deal with the natural bread that we need to live; the natural food and meat that gives our bodies strength. We are talking about the finances that are needed to pay the bills and the blessings of God that give us more than we need. It is what enables us to live in not just in the moment, but in His abundant supply.

The things that we need on a daily basis should be a point of prayer. We need to recognize where our blessings come from, but we should not pray from a place of panic or anxiety. Just after Matthew's account of the Lord's Prayer, Jesus teaches on real life and daily living.

He knew the disciples would have times of both great supply and times of need. He told them that they should not be concerned or worried about the food or clothes they would need.

> "Look at the birds, they neither sow nor reap, nor gather into barns but your heavenly Father feeds them. Are you not of more value than they?" (Matthew 6:25)

Jesus gave the disciples a promise; a promise we can take hold of and believe for our lives. If we seek first the kingdom of God, (which is the essence of the Lord's Prayer) and if we lay our lives down and live for Jesus, (which is a life of sacrifice and obedience) then there will never be a need to worry about provision. All that we need for the day, the mission, and the call will be given to us. There is no need to be concerned about provision for the day as it is taken care of. There is no need to be anxious about tomorrow's need because the same God who proved faithful today is ready to supply your needs for tomorrow. (Matthew 6:33-34)

Let us position ourselves in prayer as privileged sons and daughters with a promise from heaven. We do not have to live in a "hope" that God has heard our cry and will answer. We can live in the knowledge that God already intends to move and meet the daily needs of His children.

Let's look at a few examples by starting with the time that Jesus fed a few thousand hungry people. Most people know the story. Jesus had taught the people all day and it was getting late. The people were hungry, but Jesus and the disciples didn't have the means to feed them. All they had was the offering of a small boy who willingly gave his five loaves and two fish.

> Then He commanded the multitude to sit down on the grass. And He took the five loaves and the two fish, and looking up to heaven, He blessed and broke and gave the loaves to the disciples; and the disciples gave to the multitude. (Matthew 14:19)

This large group of people came out to hear the teachings of Jesus and they had been filled with spiritual food, but now they were hungry for natural bread. I love how Jesus responds because we sometimes find ourselves in a place where we think we can live and fly high on the spiritual and we don't need the natural. Jesus knew that they and we need both.

Jesus had the disciples seat all of the people. He did this in faith because in that moment, there was not enough food to give them. In fact, He probably had just enough to feed a family. He had them seated in a place of expectation. They didn't know how much food or how little Jesus had, but they were led to believe that they would be fed. That which Jesus carried, an expectation that God would meet their need, was activated in the multitude. He seated them with the intention to feed them. They sat with the intention of being fed.

Jesus took what He had and blessed it. He didn't complain that there was not enough, neither did he hold back the little he had for himself and the disciples. Jesus believed that the same heavenly Father who brought the boy with five loaves and two fish would also increase what He had given. He who had begun this good work would be faithful to complete it.

It is dangerous to look at the need and reduce our belief to what we have in our hands. What we have in the present will often fall short to that which we need. What we have is just a starting point; a place of faith and thanksgiving.

Jesus took the bread and fish and looked up to heaven. He realized that the miracle and the increase would be supernatural. He did not first offer what He had to those seated, but to God the Father who would bless and increase it. As the bread was broken, it multiplied. There is such a powerful truth in the breaking process. As painful as it is, the place that we often feel broken is the place that God works and increases the most. There are many times when we give from a place of abundance, but how often do we give from a place of brokenness, trusting God to move?

As the meal was blessed, broken and given, so heaven responded and multiplied that which they had. Not only were all of the people fed, but there were twelve full baskets remaining. Was this a sign to the disciples, a basket for each of the twelve? Was this an indication that God would continue to supply their needs? Or was it simply the fact that God doesn't always just supply enough, but gives more?

We move from a place of need and supply to a place of abundance. When the crowd sat down, they were hungry. After God moved and supplied bread and fish as a meal, they all ate and were filled. Their hunger and need was for a moment, but the testimony that they had received was bread from heaven and was a lifetime message.

The disciples should not have been surprised at this miracle because the way that they first met Jesus was through miraculous provision. Jesus had been preaching the gospel of the kingdom and the crowd was pressed against Him. When He looked up, He saw two boats and got in one which belonged to the fisherman, Simon Peter. He asked him to push out from the shore a little.

Now Jesus had stepped into a boat that was meant to be filled with fish, but there were no fish! It had been a bad night and the fisherman had caught nothing. Their daily need had not been met.

Jesus instructs them to push back out into the deep and to cast out their nets again. They had already been doing this all night. They were tired. What hope did they have that this trip would produce what they needed? The difference this time was that Jesus was in the boat.

We know the story. Jesus instructs them where to cast their nets and they have an almighty catch. It was so big that their nets were breaking. It stretched them to capacity. They caught more than they could have hoped for or imagined. This was the kind of catch that fishermen dreamed about. (Luke 5:1-11)

I know that the greater part of this story is the fact that Jesus met some fisherman and blew their minds. In so doing, He called them to be fishers of men. They had experienced a miracle and believed that Jesus was the Christ. They left all they had and followed Jesus and became the fishers of men that He promised they would become. Yet, the foundation of them believing was the fact that He provided their daily need and much more.

Sometimes our daily provision comes by us allowing Jesus to get into our boat or our place of work. It's the place of allowing Him to instruct us in what we are already doing. Part of this is the realization that we may be good at what we do, but with Jesus, we can be better. As we learn to listen and obey, so we see supernatural increase. This is the part of us that allows or invites the kingdom of

God to not only influence our life, but all that we touch and all that we do.

The moment we give the boat, business, or job to Jesus we create a place for the supernatural to be released. Creative insight takes place. We get ideas and wisdom on how to do what we are doing in a better or more productive way. This is truly the place that we experience the supernatural "power to get wealth, that He may establish covenant." (Deuteronomy 8:18) This is not just for us to enjoy, but we become a vessel that God moves provision through for others. It is that which God gives for us to enjoy and to bless others.

The disciples didn't know that Jesus was going to get in their boat that day. It was a day that not only met their need, but changed their destiny. When we pray for God to give us our daily bread, we invite Him into our boat. We need to listen to His instruction. You might receive more than you had bargained for. You will receive your daily bread but you may also experience a change of direction in your life.

Miracle Money

One of my favorite stories of provision is when the "tax man" came to Peter looking for the temple tax. We all know about the tax man. He is always looking for his portion. I guess the good news is that if you owe a lot, it is because you have made a lot of money. Whether you pay your taxes weekly, monthly, or at the end of the year, you will have to pay them.

The tax man created a discussion between Peter and Jesus. Peter wanted to know if they were required to pay the temple tax. (Just a note, this was a different tax than that which was required by Rome.)

The part of the story I want us to see is the way that God provided the money to pay the taxes.

Jesus took a fisherman to go fishing. The purpose was not to catch fish to trade with nor was it to reveal the fisherman's ability to catch fish to use as a resource. It was not about his skill or how many fish he could catch. He just needed to catch one fish.

I think Jesus uses this example because when needs arise, we automatically do what we know to do or what we have been trained to do. We try to make a way to pay the bill with the skills or knowledge we have. So Jesus, in a strange twist, allows the fisherman to catch one fish. It would not be enough to trade or to pay the temple tax. However, the supernatural element would be discovered in what Jesus did with Peter's fishing skills.

As he caught the fish, the first and only fish, their need was met. They opened the fish's mouth and discovered a coin. This was enough money to pay the taxes for both Jesus and Peter. (Matthew 17:24-27)

Daily provision may come through people, but you may also discover money in your wallet that was not there before. It may be that you receive a raise at work or it could be a check in the mail. It is important not to limit God or try to know how He will move. We just need to be confident that God will move.

In this story, we see that the temple tax was not a need yesterday. In fact, as they awoke on that day, it was not a need. It was one of those things that just happened; it was out of the blue. It presented itself like a car breaking down or an unexpected bill. This became their daily need. The need created a place for a supernatural miracle to take place which was something that Peter had never seen before. This was an invitation into a new dimension of receiving gifts from heaven. Don't let those sudden unexpected bills steal your peace. Get ready to go on a new supernatural adventure with Jesus. When faced with an unexpected need, expect an unexpected miracle to take place.

Increased Capacity Leads to Greater Prosperity

There are times in our lives when we experience a greater need than other times. In the midst of those challenges, we may feel abandoned. It may seem like God has not heard our cry. How could things get so bad?

It's not that God has not heard your cry, but He is allowing a season in which the need is greater. The greater need increases our capacity to receive a greater blessing.

Let me show you how this works. There is a woman in the Old Testament whose husband was a prophet. The prophet dies and leaves the women in debt. We all know how crippling debt can be. It can bring shame, depression, and at times, a feeling of just wanting to give up. This woman's debt was so deep that the creditors were coming to take her sons as slaves.

In a desperate plea, she cries out to Elisha. She can no longer keep this private, personal matter to herself. She is desperate!

Elisha asks the woman what she has in her home; how can she help herself? She responds by telling the prophet that she has nothing of significance, just a little oil. She placed no value in what she had. It didn't seem like enough to make a difference in the face of such a great problem. Life had beaten her down. However, the prophet Elisha knew that this small amount of oil in the hands of God could be turned into a great blessing.

He instructs the sons to borrow vessels, as many as they could get. He wanted to enlarge their thinking. He was increasing their capacity to contain the blessing that was coming. He didn't want their thinking to be reduced to a "just enough" mentality. He wanted them to know that God could not only supply the need at hand, but turn their entire lives around.

As they gathered the vessels, their capacity to fill the jars with oil increased. Once they had all the jars they could find, they were instructed to fill them with the oil. The oil continued to be poured into the vessels supernaturally. Every vessel was filled. The woman brought the little she had and God used her little to do a great work.

Once the vessels were filled, the prophet told the sons to sell the oil, pay their debt, and live on the rest. Their lives were supernaturally changed. They went from a crippling need to a place of prosperity. (2 Kings 4:1-7)

We read this story and see God's great supply. The thing that God changed was not just the amount of oil that they had, but their capacity to receive all that He wanted to give them.

Many people will find themselves in a place of need. The same people have great promises of God, visions that will impact communities or even nations. What they need is far beyond what they have. In fact, what they have is not even enough to live on. In this moment of praying "give us this day our daily bread," God is increasing our capacity. That which seems like it is reducing us to debt and lack is actually a place in which God is increasing our capacity.

Our daily need is a supernatural seedbed for provision. Our daily provision increases our capacity to trust in God for both our family's needs and the God-given dreams we carry. Don't allow the size of your need to devalue you as an individual or reduce the size of your dream. Trust in God should not be reduced by our circumstances, but elevated by His promises. God has promised to meet your daily need.

God Supplies the Seed

As I continue to think about God's miracles and daily supply, I cannot help but think about the law of sowing and reaping. I know the Bible is clear. What a man sows, he shall reap. I believe in giving my tithes and offerings. I believe in being obedient to the leading of the Holy Spirit in helping others in need. I have seen God honor that which I have given many times. I have experienced His increase and provision. But for me, the starting place of increase comes from God and not man.

As much as I believe in this process of sowing and reaping, we are often told that God gives to us because we have given to Him. This is great truth, but the process starts with God giving to us. All that we can give and do for others starts in the heart and actions of God. It actually starts with us receiving from Him so we can give back to Him and to others.

Our love for others is created by His love for us. Our ability to worship comes from an intimate place where we have heard the whispers of His heart and love toward us as He rejoices over us. What we have received from God creates a flow or river of grace, not only into our lives, but through our lives. As we have freely received so we freely give back to God and to others. With this in mind, we start to understand that our ability to give to others or to a church or mission is possible because God first gave us our daily bread.

And God is able to make all grace abound towards you, that you always having all sufficiency in all things, may have an abundance for every good work. As it is written "He has dispersed abroad, He has given to the poor, His righteousness endures forever." Now may He who supplies seed to the sower, and bread for food, supply and multiply the seed you have sown and increase the fruits of your righteousness. (2 Corinthians 9:8-10)

The Father wants us to put our trust in Him to provide our daily bread. That which we receive becomes our seed. The process of sowing and reaping starts with God. This may be a job that He has given or a new opportunity He has opened for us. It could be a check in the mail or supernatural provision from an unknown source. However we receive our seed, starts with God's desire to give us our daily bread. It is from that which we have received that we can then start to give back to Him and to others. Never consume all your harvest or seed. If you do, you will not have the seed you need for your next harvest.

God's Great Delight

Whenever we receive something miraculous from God it creates great delight. It is in these moments that we want to shout for joy. We sing with thanksgiving. Some of us really get our groove on as we dance around the house and scream about how good God is!

I believe the joy and delight we are feeling is also exhibited by the Father. This moment is not lost on Him. This is an opportunity for the Father to rejoice in our needs being met. I don't think we are the only ones doing the happy dance. I think the Father is also rejoicing as He supplies our need and experiences our joy.

Let them shout for joy and be glad, who favor my righteous cause; And let them say continually, "Let the Lord be magnified, who has <u>pleasure in the prosperity</u> of His servants. (Psalm 35:27)

Like any good earthly father, God takes pleasure or delight when his children prosper. King David, the author of this psalm or song, tells us to shout for joy. Sing it out, magnify the Lord. We should be glad when we experience God's blessing. The dark season of the soul or time of longing has been transformed into a time of receiving. Our prayer has been answered and you are not the only one doing the happy dance.

This gets better because Jesus tells us that this can and should be a daily experience. We can come every day and ask for our daily bread.

Spiritual Bread

How often do we hear our children tell us throughout the day that they are hungry? It feels like they are always searching for something to eat. Their growing bodies crave food in order to sustain their growth. They need their daily bread.

In a similar way, we as children of God should be craving spiritual food. We should have a daily hunger to connect with and hear from our Father in heaven.

Our daily bread is not just natural food or provision, but spiritual food that is needed to feed our spirit man. It is the very Word of God, the bread of life that gives us what we need to grow and survive as believers.

When Jesus instructed the disciples to pray "give us this day our daily bread," He was encouraging them to rely on the Father for more than just natural bread. He wanted them to experience provision on both a natural and supernatural level.

After Jesus had been baptized, He was led by the Holy Spirit into the wilderness. After fasting for forty days, Jesus became hungry. This is not a normal hunger. This is not like being an hour late for dinner or missing lunch. Jesus had not eaten for not just days or weeks, but for over a month. He was probably exhausted, tired, and feeling weak. It's not surprising that the devil sought this as an opportunity to turn up and try to tempt Him. The enemy often attacks us when we are tired or weak. (Matthew 4:1-3, Luke 4:1-2)

In the midst of Jesus' tiredness, the enemy tries to tempt Jesus to turn a stone or rock into bread. He wanted Jesus to prove who He was. In the response Jesus gave, there is no suggestion that He could not have done what the devil had asked him to do, but it was not the right thing to do in that moment. Jesus responds to the devil:

"It is written, man shall not live by bread alone but by every word that proceeds from the mouth of God." (Luke 4:4)

Jesus quoted the Word of God, a scripture from the Old Testament to disarm the devil's temptation. Let's read that scripture:

"So He humbled you, allowed you to be hungry, and fed you with manna which you did not know nor did your fathers know, that He might make you know that man shall not live by bread alone; but man lives by every word that proceeds from the mouth of the Lord." (Deuteronomy 8:3)

Jesus used the Old Testament scripture that declares how God sustained His children in the wilderness. Every day, God provided them with manna or angel food. When we read this scripture, we come to understand that the natural was just a sign of how God wanted to sustain them with spiritual food. His desire was that they would be fed both naturally and spiritually. This scripture connects the natural food or manna with "every word that proceeds out of the mouth of God." Israel would not only rely on the Father for daily bread from heaven, but they would come to rely on Him for a daily impartation of revelation. He wanted them to hunger for the word of God. The revelation to them was that He would meet their spiritual hunger for the word just has He had met their natural hunger with manna from heaven.

This scripture in Luke 4:4 refers to bread as daily food as seen in the manna and the words of God. When Jesus faced the devil, He responded with this because what he needed in that moment was not natural food, but the word of God. When Jesus told His disciples to pray, "Give us this day our daily bread," He was referring to both natural food and the word of God or the bread of life.

We should be as hungry to receive a daily word from God as we are for natural bread.

When we continue to read about how the devil tempted Jesus, we see that in every case Jesus responded by using the Word of God as a weapon against the devil. He used Old Testament scripture to fight back every attack of the enemy.

I believe that with each attack, the Father in heaven whispered a scripture into the heart of Jesus. The voice of the Father was louder than the temptations of the enemy. Jesus used His daily bread to both sustain His spiritual condition and to overcome the temptations of the enemy.

When we examine this closer, we see that with the first temptation, the devil wanted Jesus to prove who He was. He taunted Jesus, wanting Him to prove that He was the Son of God. He desired to get Him to act out of pride!

His identity was under attack. The devil was questioning who He was. "Are you really the Son of God?" How often has the devil questioned who you are? I have written about this scripture before in my book Awakening the Issachar Generation, so I don't want to repeat all that I wrote before. However, I do want to highlight how Jesus responded: "Man shall not live by bread alone but by every word that proceeds out of the mouth of God".

This response causes me to ask what was the last thing that proceeded out of the mouth of the Father toward Jesus? We find the answer at His baptism:

> When all the people were baptized, it came to pass that Jesus also was baptized; and while He prayed, the heavens were opened and the Holy Spirit descended upon Him, and a voice came from heaven which said, "You are my beloved Son, In You I am well pleased." (Luke 3:21-22)

The last word that Jesus received was "You are my beloved Son." The first temptation questioned Jesus' sonship. When Jesus said that man should not live by bread alone but by every word that proceeds out of the mouth of God, He was remembering the last word the Father had given Him. This was truly spiritual manna or bread from heaven.

Jesus disarmed the enemy by remembering both the prophetic word of God that was pronounced by the Father at His baptism and by using the written Word of God from the Old Testament. Jesus was sustained and fed with supernatural daily bread that He used to defeat every lie and attack of the enemy.

I think it's also interesting to see that the Father did not speak or send the Holy Spirit until Jesus had unlocked heaven through prayer. (Luke 3:21) Let me put it this way; when we pray, we open the connection between heaven and earth. We are inviting heaven to invade earth. In that moment, we are ready to receive bread or the word of God from heaven. It's the word of God that sustains, nourishes, and enable us to overcome.

Let's put this into the context of praying with God. Our prayer life becomes fueled by the very words that we receive from God. God speaks to us and we use what He says to pray. His words may come as a still small voice or a bold statement of intent. It may be a calm response to the storm we are in or words of promise and declaration that we use as a weapon of warfare. When the Father speaks, He sets our feet on a firm foundation. Like Jesus, we can use the very words to overcome that which is in front of us.

When God speaks, it both steadies the ship in a storm and sets the direction of our journey for that day or season. God uses both the things that are written in the Word of God and the words that He places in our hearts to feed us and lead us. "Every word that proceeds out of the mouth of God" is our daily bread.

If you are praying about one thing and God is not speaking to you, pause for a moment. Change your approach. Ask the Father what He wants to talk to you about. Allow Him to move your heart so your prayers become fueled by His word. This opens up a whole new area of prayer. We stop praying from our own wants and instead invite God's desires for our day.

When God speaks, "His words are like honey on our lips." (Psalm 119:103) They don't just sustain us, they are sweet to taste. His words are meant to become our words, which in turn become like honey on our lips. They are full of life and hope.

When prayer starts with our words, it can often feel heavy. But the moment we receive our daily bread and we hear God speak, everything changes. His word becomes a "light in the darkness and a lamp to our feet." That which we could not see is now illuminated before us. We gain a different perspective. The darkness gives way to the light of the word and we see clearly. We pray differently because we are now praying with God and not just to God. We have heard His heartbeat. We are now praying in unity and agreement with the Father.

How hungry are you for spiritual daily bread? It amazes me how many people are happy to eat from another person's table or even from their leftovers. What I mean is that we can become happy and sustained by the preaching, teaching, or revelation that others receive. It is easy to hear a good message on many multimedia platforms and be satisfied. It's good that we can receive the word from many different places and be encouraged. But how awesome would it be if you had an expectation for God to talk to you daily; that every day you could receive the bread He wants to give you?

God wants to speak to you today. He has created us as sheep to hear the voice of the shepherd. Sheep do not have strong natural sight, but do have great hearing. They know the sound, the footsteps, and the voice of the shepherd that both protects and leads them. We are like sheep that put our trust in the shepherd's voice. We are not to be distracted by what we see around us because natural sheep are not to be led by what they see, but by what they hear. That which is happening in the natural can steal your peace. It's time to hear the voice of the good shepherd, receive His daily bread, and hear what God is saying this day.

When we pray, "Give us this day our daily bread" we are positioning ourselves to receive the bread from heaven; the very words of the Father. We are no longer just using our words to pray to God, but we hear His words and pray with God, our Father.

I Can Smell the Bread

I love the smell of hot bread from the bakery. It reminds me of time that I have spent in Mediterranean cities. You wake up in the morning to the smell of fresh hot bread. It calls your name, it gets you out of bed and you can't wait to taste what's cooking. The aroma is enticing; it grabs hold of your senses and you desire bread!

If I can say it this way, I can smell the bread in the same way that Elijah heard "the sound of abundance of rain." In this Old Testament story, it has not rained in Israel for three and half years and suddenly the prophet hears "the sound of abundance of rain." He hears something before he has seen a cloud or felt a raindrop. There is a confidence that he has been heard and rain is on the way. If you have read the story you will know that shortly after, the rain came.

James, in the New Testament, refers to this story:

> " ...... The effective fervent prayer of a righteous man avails much. Elijah was a man, with a nature like ours, and he prayed earnestly that it would not rain; and it did not rain on the land for three years and six months. And he prayed again, and the heavens gave rain, and the earth produced its fruit." (James 5:16-18)

Elijah "heard the sound of abundance" before abundance came. What he heard caused a fervent prayer which availed much. In a similar way, I can smell the bread, both natural and spiritual. It is time for the church to smell the bread. What is it that you have heard from heaven? What is the sound that's reverberating in your heart? Allow His word to move you in daily prayer. His word becomes your heartbeat. You are no longer just praying your prayers but you have partnered with and are praying in relationship with the Father. You are positioned and poised to receive your daily bread. It is that bread, natural and spiritual, that will not only meet your need, but also the needs of all those you are in relationship with or come in contact with.

Let's take what God has given us in "Our daily bread" and break it. See it multiply as heaven invades earth.

Chapter 7: Forgiven and Forgive

Forgive us our debt (sins.) As we forgive our debtors. (Matthew 6.12)

There is no greater power than forgiveness. The gospel hinges on it, the kingdom is founded in it, and the Father's love is revealed through it.

When we read the Bible we discover that it's a book of redemption. It is the unfolding revelation of God's love toward people who have fallen short of the perfection of God's righteousness. From Genesis to Revelation, we see how often man fails but God continues to reach out and rescue them from their own self destruction.

This picture of forgiveness is probably best captured in the parable of the lost son. I can just imagine a smile breaking out on the face of Jesus as He told the story of the prodigal son and the love of the Father.

He prodded the hearts of the listeners with the reality that we are all prodigals. We have all chosen to do our own thing and go our own way. Then, a life crisis happens and it causes us to look for answers. We reevaluate where we are and how we have come to find ourselves in a place of despair.

We realize that we have foolishly tried to live independently of the Father's love and guidance. In our desperation, we recognize our fault and come crawling back to the Father; repenting, confessing, and sometimes groveling. We are looking for a second, third, or thirtieth chance to change. Like the prodigal son, our expectation is minimal. We grovel like a slave, hoping for just enough grace to be accepted. We need forgiveness again and we hope we will be given another chance to live differently.

What we are met with is unashamed, unbridled, extravagant love. The Father is not just hoping that one day we will come back to Him, but with great expectation He is waiting for us. As soon as we show a sign that our hearts are open, He runs toward us. With open arms and sloppy kisses, He accepts us. He quickly deals with our slave-like groveling and rewards us with total forgiveness.

Forgiveness turns to redemption as He restores us as sons and daughters of the King. He removes the feelings of shame by clothing us in royal garments that speak of who we are in Him. He places a signet ring on our hand which carries the authority of the kingdom. He dresses our feet with shoes, declaring that we are no longer slaves, but sons and daughters. The debt or chains of our sins and mistakes have been removed. We are forgiven, accepted, reunited, and restored. We are reminded that we are joint heirs with Christ Jesus and part of the kingdom of God.

At some point in the journey of life we get a glimpse, a thought, or revelation of the love of God. It's this love that draws us to Him. It's this love that awakens our hearts in times of need and desperation. It's a love that tugs at our heart when we are going in a wrong direction. It is a love that was so powerfully demonstrated when He gave His only begotten Son, Jesus, to us as gift from heaven.

It is the love of God that leads to repentance. It's the love of God that captivates our heart and draws us close to Him. It is the love of God that causes us to repent or recognize our sins, the wrong decisions we have made, and ask for forgiveness.

His forgiveness is so overwhelmingly beautiful it catches us by surprise. We are filled with grace that's undeserved but welcomed and embraced. It makes us want to turn our lives around. We desire to live differently. The same grace that covers our sins and removes the stain of unrighteous living gives us the power to live differently.

This grace is so powerful it permeates our entire being. We are not able to keep it to ourselves. The grace and forgiveness we have received, we have to give away. This starts in prayer as we forgive others as we have experienced forgiveness in our lives.

Forgive Us

I find it fascinating that the "forgive us" part of the Lord's Prayer is not the first thing Jesus told the disciples to do. In fact, when He taught them how to pray, there is a long list of things they were to recognize and pray before they got to the "forgive us" section of prayer.

This challenges my theology and understanding. As a young believer, I was told that the first thing you should do when praying was to repent of your sins. It was to make sure your heart was "right" or clean so that there was no barrier between you and God.

In understanding this, I know that much of this statement is true, but when I read the Lord's Prayer, I recognize that it's not the first thing the disciples or we are instructed to pray as believers. Now, before you close this book because what I'm saying is in opposition with your understanding, just read on a little as I explain and expound the scriptures.

When Jesus started to preach the gospel of the kingdom, the first thing He did was call people to repentance.

> From that time Jesus began to preach and say, "Repent, for the Kingdom is at hand." (Matthew 4:17)

As we go through the gospels, we see this statement of "repentance" many times. We know we have to ask for forgiveness to receive the kingdom of God.

I, like you, believe that the only way into the kingdom of God starts with Jesus. The Father's love is first demonstrated by sending His Son to die on our behalf. He is the lamb without blemish. He is our redemption. A price had to be paid for our freedom from sin and what a great price was paid. We have been purchased, not with silver or gold, but with the precious blood of Jesus.

The apostle Paul says in the book of Romans that we have to "Believe in our heart and confess with our mouth that Jesus is Lord" to be saved. The only way to the Father is through Jesus Christ.

Our salvation starts when we receive the Father's gifts. We recognize all that was given to us through Christ and all He has done for us in His sacrifice upon the cross. This leads us to repent of our sins. We apologize for living life the way we chose to live. We ask forgiveness and receive grace through Christ. In this, we surrender our lives to Jesus and we are saved.

In the Word of Jesus, repentance is the key that leads to the kingdom. It's the start of the process. Yet, when we read the Lord's Prayer, it's not the first thing we are called to pray for. Why is this?

When Jesus was teaching the disciples how to pray, they had already become believers. They had recognized Jesus as the promised Son of God or the Messiah. They had already given up everything to live for Christ. At this point of learning how to pray, they were already in the kingdom of God.

The value and importance of confession or asking for forgiveness doesn't change. It is still just as necessary after our salvation as it was before our salvation. It's what keeps our relationship in the best possible condition with the Father, but positionally, we have changed.

The disciples at this point were already in the kingdom. They were not on the outside looking for a savior, but on the inside learning to walk or live in a new way. They were no longer slaves, they were sons. So when Jesus taught them to pray, they were already praying from a different position. They had already gone through the process of repentance to receive the kingdom of God.

So I, like you, believe that repentance is part of the process that leads to the kingdom of God. Now that you are in the kingdom, you can pray for the kingdom to come. You can also pray for all of the other components in the Lord's Prayer that come before the "forgive us" portion. You are already forgiven. You are sons and daughters of the King. You can come boldly into His presence because you have accepted the blood of Christ that was shed for you.

As a believer, you can't become more righteous in your position as a son or daughter than you already are. You have been made righteous by and through Christ. This has given you the keys of the kingdom. You have been adopted into the family of God. However, when we are in the presence of God, we experience conviction. These are areas of our lives that suddenly come into focus. They need to change, have an upgrade, or we need to be transformed in our thinking and therefore our lifestyle. We recognize that these are interfering in our relationship with the Father. There is something wrong with our attitude or walk. As we recognize and ask for forgiveness, we receive grace to be forgiven and live differently.

Just before the crucifixion, Jesus was teaching the disciples about the Holy Spirit. What was He coming to do in both the world and among believers? This gives us insight into this very topic of repentance and conviction.

> "And when He (the Holy Spirit) has come, He will _convict the_ _world of sin_, and of righteousness, and of judgement: of sin, because they do not believe in Me; of righteousness, because I go to My Father and you see me no more; of judgement because the ruler of this world is judged. I still have many things to say to you, but you cannot bear them now. However, when He, the Spirit of truth, has come, _He will guide you into_ _all truth;_ for He will not speak on His own authority, but whatever He hears He will speak; and He will tell you things to come. (John 16:8-13)

I think it's easy to see that the way the Holy Spirit works in the heart of the unbeliever is different from the way He works in the believer. To the unbeliever, He comes to "convict the world of sin." Once you have come under that conviction, you repent and become a believer.

His work in the believer is to "guide them into all truth." This not only means that He leads the believer into greater revelation and vistas of truth, but that he leads us out of error. This is a truth that opposes every error, lie, deception, and work of the flesh.

In both cases, there is still a conviction and need for repentance. In the unbeliever, it's repentance, "forgive us our debt" that leads to salvation. In the believer, it's a process of continual change.

Let's come back to my original observation. "Forgive us our sins" doesn't have to be the first thing on the agenda. We would not be able to pray "Our Father in heaven" if we had not already been restored to Him through repentance. But, as sons and daughters, there is always a place of guidance, correction, and instruction in our daily walk.

It is in the protective relationship of praying "Our Father" that we can come with confidence and ask for forgiveness. His loving presence provides a place of true transparency. It is this transparency that leads to greater intimacy in our relationship with God. In His presence, we know that His love will lead to repentance. His desire for us to go from glory to glory will at times bring correction.

You may feel that this is a minor point; that the place in our prayer in which we confess our sins and repent is trivial. I, on the other hand, think it's important. Many people, even after they have become believers, struggle with an intimate relationship with the Father. They always feel unworthy. They struggle to shake the shame or remove the stain of their memories from past sins. So, every time they pray, they come to the Father in fear and trembling.

When we become believers, we are to accept by faith the sacrifice Christ made for us. Salvation is by faith and not works, not even works of prayer. More prayer does not bring more forgiveness. We have to accept that we are forgiven.

The truth I believe Jesus was establishing in the Lord's Prayer is a new relationship with the Father. It is within this relationship that we ask Him to "forgive us our sins." How many times does a child have to apologize for a mistake they have made in order to be accepted and forgiven by their earthly father? Yet, a child who knows he is already forgiven feels safe to share his failings.

I know that my children will make many mistakes. They will make wrong decisions and say things that are offensive. It is wrong to just let bad habits go. There is a need to parent, to guide, and at times, to discipline.

How we do that is in an environment of love that creates a safe place in which they can share or confess. The first thing we establish is that we love them, which is not a response to their words or actions, but is from our hearts. When we wake up, the first thing we tell them is that we love them. The last thing we do before they go to bed is tell them we love them. This is reinforced through gestures, hugs, and words throughout the day. The message of love is reinforced more than any other message.

So when they mess up, which they will do, they can be free to share. Even though they know we may be disappointed and we may not agree with the decision they have made, they also know we love them. The place of transparency that leads to greater intimacy is an environment of love. It is in this place that we can both embrace them and correct them.

As sons and daughters, we are in the household of faith. The Lord's Prayer is established in "our Father." It is from this position as sons and daughters that we are safe to confess all that is in our hearts. We know that He will lead us into greater forgiveness and freedom.

Our Nature is Transformed by His Nature

We are influenced by those who we spend time with. The more time you spend in the presence of a person, the more you become like them.

This is also true in our relationship with God. The more time we spend in the presence of God, the more we are changed. Our thinking is transformed by His words. Our nature becomes more like His nature. The way we see the world, others, and the future is through eyes of faith and not fear.

King David said that we live in a dry and thirsty land, a land without water. He was in need of being refreshed. So he looked to God in the sanctuary as his source of life and power. (Psalm 63:1) If we remain in the world without the presence of God, we will be influenced by the environment in which we live. We will become thirsty. Our spirit will be in need of spiritual water. However, if we seek God, we will find a place of refreshment. This shows us that we are influenced and changed by the place we are in or by the people with whom we spend time.

In the natural, my father is my hero. I love to spend time with him. There are many things that I want to become because of the example he is to me. This is also true of our heavenly Father. We are changed in His presence.

In the Lord's Prayer, "Our Father" is the introduction to an environment in which we are changed by His presence. The invitation of "thy kingdom come" is where we surrender our kingdom or castle for His rule and reign. When we pray "let your will be done" we are relinquishing our will for His plans and purpose in our lives. Then we come to the place of "forgive us our sins." If there is a place of transformation, this is it. This is not driven by fear of

138

expulsion or punishment because we have already come into salvation through Christ. This is a desire to be more like our Father in heaven.

There is a conviction that captivates us when we come in the presence of God. We realize that we are still in a process of change. There is a desire to be holy because He is holy. It's not a conviction that comes to punish us, but to promote us. It is a conviction that causes us to become more like Him. This continual transformation is like clay in the potter's hands. We are being transformed into vessels of honor. We are being made ready to be used in a greater way.

When we pray "forgive us our sins," we are asking for a repositioning. We are inviting correction and instruction on how we are to live. We are making ourselves ready for an upgrade in life.

We can see this happen in the life of the prophet Isaiah (Isaiah 6). I love this picture of the presence of God. The prophet is caught up to a place where he is able to see beyond the veil. This is an invisible veil that separates the natural and the supernatural. The prophet sees the presence of God and the train of His robe filling the temple.

Isaiah sees these magnificent angelic beings, the seraphim, in the presence of God. They are singing about the holiness of the Lord and proclaiming that His glory fills the earth.

Isaiah is a righteous man. He is given access to see the glory of God. Yet in the presence of the Lord, he is affected by the environment. No matter how holy he is, in the presence of a holy God he is called to give an account or is called to a higher place of holiness.

This is not a place of condemnation, but a place that is calling him higher. The prophet is convicted and confesses that he is a man who is undone in the presence of the Lord; a man who has unclean lips.

This does not mean he went around cussing, it's just a revelation in the presence of God that he could do better. He realizes his humanity in the presence of a divine God.

The moment he confesses his weakness, there is something that's released from heaven. The moment we come to our Father and confess an area of weakness or sin, it releases a gift from heaven. This gift may be a word, a promise, a tool we can use to change, or a supernatural experience that brings transformation.

As Isaiah remained in the presence of God, an angel came to him with a live coal. He touched the prophet's mouth and declared, "His iniquity is taken away and your sin is removed." In that moment, the prophet experienced the grace of God and he is repositioned for an upgrade in his walk and ministry.

When his sin is dealt with, he hears the voice of the Lord saying "Whom shall I send and who will go for us?" The prophet responds to the Lord with, "Here I am, send me." This process repositioned Isaiah to become the man that God had called him to be. God touched the very lips that He would use to speak through him to the people of Israel.

This encounter in the presence of God was to bring the promotion of God's purposes and release the prophet into the place of His calling.

When we come to our Father and pray "forgive us our sins," we are inviting Him to change us from the inside out. We have a desire to become more like Him. We are also being repositioned for the purposes of God.

I know that conviction and confession is an ongoing process. I also know that God often uses us despite our weaknesses and failings in the flesh. However, this is not an excuse to keep doing what we do in ignorance or in the name of "grace." Once an area of sin is revealed to us, we should do all we can to change it. Once confession takes place, we invite supernatural help from heaven to help us change. The same grace of God that covers our sin is the grace that gives us the power to change and transform our lives.

The reason that "sin" is translated as "debt" in some versions of the Lord's Prayer is because it has a deeper meaning. It reveals that our sins hold us indebted or enslaved in an area of our lives. Someone or something has us chained. This restricts us from being who we have been created to be. Jesus came to set the captive free. He wants you free of all that enslaves you. Jesus has broken the chains that hold you back from being who God intended and called you to become.

Get into the presence of God as often as you can. You will be changed by His presence. It may not all happen overnight, but the more time we spend with Him, the more we are changed by Him.

Conviction that leads to confession starts with a picture of how God sees us. You and I are to reflect the presence of God. We are not to be hidden, but are to be on display reflecting as a mirror the image of the glory of God. We are being and will continue to be transformed from glory to glory by the Spirit, the person and power of God. (2 Corinthians 3:18)

Conviction, not Condemnation

There is a big difference between conviction of sin and condemnation. Conviction allows us to come boldly before the Father through the blood of Jesus. We know that the Father loves us and responds favorably to the confession of sin.

Conviction brings us to the cross and reveals Jesus who died on our behalf. It is in this place that we also die to self and to the desires of our flesh. We have been encouraged by Christ to take up our cross daily. Like in the Lord's Prayer, we should practice confession as a place of freedom. It is at the cross that we die, but it is also the place that we discover resurrection life.

When the Holy Spirit brings conviction in our lives, it is always with a road map of promises. He paints a picture of who we are in Christ and who we are becoming in our walk with God. Conviction creates a way to navigate through our errors and into complete freedom.

Condemnation may look and sound like God, but it is not. It is a counterfeit of the real thing. It is not sourced by love, but by hate. Its aim is to bind you and keep you held captive in your sin. The orchestrator of condemnation is the father of lies, the devil.

The devil will remind you of your sins to shame you, to break you, and to hold you captive by them. He wants you to live under the cloud of rejection and bitterness. He loves for you to carry a victim mentality, always living in a place of discouragement. Condemnation reveals your innermost struggles without hope of freedom. The devil condemns you to a life without breakthrough. He declares that you're done, it's over, and there is no bright future.

This is a lie. The scripture declares or even shouts out in the face of the lies of the enemy:

> There is therefore now no condemnation to those who are in Christ Jesus, who do not walk according to the flesh but according to the Spirit. (Romans 8:1)

Conviction not only brings us face to face with our sins, failings, and weakness, it simultaneously reminds us of the transforming power of God. It is the grace of God that exchanges who we are with who He is for us and who He is in us.

Condemnation aims to separate you from God as it tries to force a wedge into our relationship. Conviction reminds us that we cannot live this life on our own, but only in harmony with the Father.

Condemnation will tell you that at every failing, God will leave you. Conviction reminds us that in every failing, God has a solution to lead us from victim to victory. God is there on our journey, holding us by the hand and guiding us into a better future.

Correction is not Rejection

As we continue our journey in the Lord's Prayer, we discover that "forgive us our sins" may come from a place of correction. Now this is scary because we live in a world where people hate to be corrected. Yet, true correction springs out of the love of God and into a better, more prosperous future.

Many have the misconception that God is always angry, mad at His children, and is ready to judge them or punish them. I obviously do not believe this and I am grateful that judgement took place on the cross.

However, to paint a picture that God never corrects His children is also misguided. It is not a true picture of God or of His love toward us.

To love and never guide is not love, it's abandonment. It says "I love you" but not enough to help you become who you have the potential to be. I have seen many parents, especially those who have gone through a divorce, try to be their children's best friends. They want to hang out and do all the cool stuff without teaching and guiding them. Their love is masked by the fear of losing their children or being rejected by them.

True love starts on a foundation of truth; the truth of how God loves us and what we have inherited through His love, but it also exposes weaknesses that lead us into error. It addresses the so called elephants in the room. It doesn't allow us to live under a mask of deceit or deception. He highlights and reveals that which is hidden in darkness and He brings it into the light. God always works in the light!

When we pray "forgive us our debts," we are sending an invitation to God. We are inviting Him to shine light into every area of our hearts. We are surrendering our lives so that any work of darkness, debt, or sin will be revealed.

When we come into a place of confession, we are met with grace. Transformation starts to take place. The problem is when we refuse to recognize our mistakes; when we walk in the pride of life and do as we please. It is when we live and continue to walk in the flesh without remorse or repentance. It is then that we learn about the correction of God.

As we look at this we must remember that correction in Jesus never brings a curse. The punishment of a curse was connected to the old covenant found in the Old Testament. This took place when the children of Israel refused to walk in the ways of God. They chose to do what they wanted to do and so under the agreement of the convent, this opened them up to a curse.

In Christ, there is no curse. The curse was removed when God made His covenant with Christ and not with man. The Bible clearly states that "all the promises of God in Him are yes, and in Him amen, to the glory of God through us." (2 Corinthians 1:20) You will notice in this verse that there is no mention of a curse.

So when correction comes, it doesn't come as a curse, but God can and will resist you. He will stop you from doing what you are doing or are meant to do. He can close the doors He had opened for you. It may bring a delay in the promises of God. When we walk in sin, we are walking in pride. We are saying that we know best or that we will do what we want to do. We are clearly told that "God resists the proud but gives grace to the humble." (1 Peter 5:5)

God resists us to catch our attention; to change the direction we are going. He knows that we are on a slippery slope of self destruction and unless it's addressed, it will get worse. James, the half-brother of Jesus, said "But each one is tempted when he is drawn away by his own desires and enticed. Then when desire has conceived, it gives birth to sin; and sin when it is full-grown, brings forth death." (James 1:14-15)

I can confidently say that every unrepented or ignored area of sin will lead to death at some point. This may not be physical death, but can be the death of a relationship, business, or dream. This is the work of the devil who comes to kill, steal, and destroy. One of the reasons the Holy Spirit convicts us of sin is because He wants to halt the destructive nature of the thing we are doing. Let's remember that Jesus came to give life and life more abundant.

In dealing with correction, the writer of the book of Hebrews says it best:

And you have forgotten the exhortation which speaks to you as sons:

"My son, do not despise the chastening of the Lord, nor be discouraged when you are rebuked by Him; For whom the Lord loves He chastens, and scourges every son He receives."

If you endure chastening, God deals with you as with sons; for what son is there whom a father does not chasten?

But if you are without chastening, of which all have become partakers, then you are illegitimate and not sons.

Furthermore, we have had human fathers who corrected us, and we paid them respect. Shall we not much more readily be in subjection to the Father of spirits and live?

For they for a few days chastened us as seemed best to them, but He for our profit, that we may be partakers of His holiness.

Now no chastening seems to be joyful for the present, but painful; nevertheless, afterwards it yields the peaceable fruit of righteousness to those who have been trained by it. (Hebrews 12:5-11)

Some in the church will point to the fact that there are a couple of examples in the New Testament in which the correction of God seems very tough. I would agree that there are a few examples of tough love and like in life, there are moments that require tough love. However, when we stand back and look at the New Testament as a whole, we are overwhelmed by the grace.

In dealing with correction, we have to remember that God loves the prodigal. He approaches us from a place of mercy and grace. Yet, He will not ignore our acts of rebellion, and at times, there is a need for tough love.

Even in these times of correction, God the Father calls out to us from a place of love. He is longing for it to lead us into repentance. He is looking for a change of lifestyle; a moment in which we turn from living life one way to living life differently. The Father's correction leads to confession. This leads us to pray "forgive us our sins." In that moment, as we humble ourselves in the presence of God, we are met with grace seen in the love of the Father that seeks to exalt the humble.

This is a powerful transformation from being resisted to being supernaturally exalted. The pride that may have held us back and delayed the promises of God is now a place of supernatural acceleration. God will restore the years the locusts have eaten. All that the enemy meant for harm and pride, God can turn for His good. Every bad decision that led to loss is changed into a place of grace and another chance to do it right. The Father's correction leads to experiences or transformation that we call testimonies and it's these testimonies that we use to overcome the devil and help others.

Benefits of Confession

There is great power in confession and praying "forgive us our debts." It not only leads to salvation through Christ, but to great freedom. It unlocks other areas of the kingdom as well. Let me share a few.

In the book of Revelation, the churches and therefore the people, were called to repentance. They received supernatural insight into the error of their ways.

In every case that they were called to repent, they were given instruction on how to change and what change looked like. They were also given a promise that if they repented, they would overcome and inherit a great blessing from God. (Revelation Chapters 2-3)

That which overcomes us in life is taken captive at the place of repentance. Then, we who have been set free become the overcomers we are destined to become.

Another benefit was seen at the start of the early church. We see the disciples calling the people to repent. Again, this not only led to their sins being forgiven, but totally removed. At this time, they were also given a promise of refreshing to accompany their repentance.

When we repent from our sins, there is no longer a barrier that keeps us out of the presence of God. In fact, there is an invitation to come into His presence and come often. It is in this place that we can experience the refreshing presence of God. This is not a one-time experience as we are called to "times" of refreshing. Come as often as you need!

> Repent therefore and be converted, that your sins may be blotted out, so that times of refreshing may come from the presence of the Lord. (Acts 3:19)

I love the work of the Holy Spirit in our lives and how He at times gently convicts us and other times strongly convicts us of sin. This conviction leads to repentance and reveals another benefit of confession. We are reminded in the book of Romans that there is "righteousness and peace and joy in the Holy Spirit." (Romans 14:17)

I see this as a progressive promise. When we are walking in righteousness, we experience peace and when we have peace, we live in a place of joy. The opposite is also true. When we walk in unrighteousness, we do not feel at peace, but we live a life of chaos. Chaos is never a good breeding ground for joy.

Let's invite the Holy Spirit to bring us to a place of confession. We want to live righteously and feel the peace of God that leads us to shout with joy. The good news is that the Holy Spirit doesn't just lead us into righteous living, He reveals who we are as the righteous of God through Christ Jesus. He reminds us of our position and inheritance. When you know who you are, it creates peace in your life. That peace is more than a feeling, but the knowledge that God is with you in all circumstances. No matter what we face, the peace we have will lead us to joy.

Finally, there are some areas of sin that keep us bound and sick. These are things that we have done or that have been done to us by other people that create anger or bitterness. Many people often keep these secrets to themselves in fear of what people might say or think.

The more we keep them hidden, the more they affect our spirit, soul, and body. We are in debt to them or we are enslaved by these secret things. Our lives will be shrouded with the guilt, shame, or worthlessness that these sins bring. The moment we confess them and bring them into the light, they lose their grip on our lives.

> *"Confess your trespasses to one another, and pray for one another, that you may be healed." (James 5:16)*

The moment we start confessing our sins and the sins of others and learn to forgive is the moment that healing takes place. This leads to "forgive us our debts, as we forgive our debtors."

Grace Reproduces Grace

This brings us to the way we pray for and respond to those who have sinned against us. There is never an excuse when others treat us poorly, but there is a kingdom response. This is not natural or at times easy, but we have to learn to forgive others just as we have been forgiven.

The model of the Father is to show grace. Grace we receive is grace that can be given away. As we are moved in awe that God can forgive us for the terrible things we have said and done, we are equally encouraged to extend that forgiveness to others. Even to our enemies.

I think we spend far too much time praying and confessing our own sins and not nearly enough time praying for those who have sinned against us. In the words of Jesus we should "pray for our enemies."

I spent a lot of time dealing with this subject in my first book, Broken: Restoration for God's Wounded. I don't want to repeat all of what I have said before, but I do want to emphasize how Jesus put this into practice with a prayer and a cry that shook the world.

How did Jesus respond and pray for His enemies when they violently arrested Him and beat Him, tearing the beard from His face? They refused to accept Him and the mission He had been called to do. They did not see that He had been sent by the Father. They mocked and called Him names as they whipped His body. They shamelessly dragged Him through the streets, nailed Him to a cross, and hung Him between thieves to die.

How did Jesus respond when those who, a few days earlier, had sung His praise and shouted hosanna in the streets? They were the same people, His own people, who He had come to. Now they rejected

Him and their tune had changed. They no longer proclaimed "hosanna" but "crucify, crucify!"

Rejected, abandoned, and denied, Jesus hung upon the cross. His dignity had been removed. He was humbled beyond recognition. Yet, with a cry and shout and with arms stretched wide, He prayed for His enemies. They were only a few short words, but powerful. In fact, so powerful that they continue to cry out and remind us of amazing grace. "Father forgive, they know not what they do!"

How could Jesus pray such a powerful prayer? It was because of the love that brought Him here. The love of the Father who gave His only begotten son for a dying world was still beating in His chest. It was alive and it cried out for the lost.

The Lord's Prayer is so powerful in leading us in a cry that asks for forgiveness for our sins. It causes us to confidently know that God will have grace toward us. Equally, it moves us with the love of the Father toward others. As we have been showered with love, so we cry out again not for ourselves, but for others.

Praying to God is coming with confessions and asking for forgiveness. We then transition from praying to God to praying with God. As we understand His heart toward us, we understand His heart toward others. We become the vehicle through which grace is received and revealed. This prayer activates the loving nature of God in us. We become the conduit through which grace is released in praying for our enemies. It moves us with compassion and mercy to cry out, call out, and reach out with love.

Chapter 8: The Great Deliverer

And do not lead us into temptation, but deliver us from the evil one.
For yours is the kingdom and the power and the glory forever. Amen.
(Matthew 6:13)

Jesus concludes the Lord's Prayer with a final call to victory. The very reason we need a savior and redeemer is because the first Adam fell at the place of temptation. This was the crack in the foundation of the fall of creation. With a choice, Adam and Eve were given the power of free will. All of God's beauty would be found at the tree of life. All they had to do was avoid the tree of knowledge of good and evil.

The temptation was subtle. The devil did not come with his face painted red or with horns and a pitch fork. He did not come with shouts and threats. In fact, he offered that which seemed reasonable and attractive.

With a twinkle in his eye and a soft smooth voice he pleaded, "Surely you will not die. Why would God not want you to possess the power of the knowledge of good and evil? He knows that in the day you eat, your eyes will be opened. You will see like never before, you will be more like God."

Like in many areas of temptation, Eve looked or gazed at the fruit and she was captivated. She was caught up with what she saw or envisioned. Her mind must have been filled with all that the devil suggested she could have and she started to believe that there would be no consequences for her decision. That which she saw seemed good to her. Eve activated free will and made her choice. With her husband standing next to her, she took the fruit and gave some to Adam. In that moment, temptation became sin and we all know the effects.

I do not believe that God necessarily wanted to keep the knowledge of good and evil from them, but this was not the time or the way He wanted them to learn these truths. I believe He would have taught them these areas of truth in His time and in the security of relationship.

God is always bringing and increasing revelation and truths in our lives. I believe this will be an ongoing experience throughout eternity. For Adam and Eve, this started in the cool of the day. For us, it started at the point we invited Jesus into our lives.

Revelation knowledge is different from earthy knowledge. One is built in relationship with God and the other through our own quest to know more. There are some things that God keeps from us until an appointed time. We can see in the New Testament that there were some things that God had kept from the angels. They didn't have a full understanding of the church and what it would look like until the church was born. The church was a mystery to them. Once unveiled, the church became a revelation of what the love and grace of God looks like.

The scripture said that we, the church, were hidden in God and not revealed until this present age. This mystery would not be seen until the church was uncovered and God's truth was taught through the church. We would make known the very things that God had kept from the angels for ages upon ages. Today, through relationship and experience, we exhibit and teach these mysteries to principalities and powers in heavenly places. (Ephesians 3:3-10)

I am sharing this because I think what was being offered to Adam and Eve was a shortcut. The enemy offered them knowledge without effort or work. They would be able to have something without the need of relationship with God. They could get this knowledge on their own and independent of God. They just had to eat the fruit!

This sounds a bit like the temptation that Jesus faced. The enemy told Him "I will give you all the kingdoms of the world. All you have to do is bow down and worship me." This would have been an easy, quick fix. It's all yours; just give me your soul!

We would all like to skip the lessons of life. No one really wants to work hard, but we all want to be millionaires. That's why the lottery is so popular.

For Adam and Eve, the shortcut was to gain in a moment the knowledge of good and evil. "Just eat and it's yours." The process cut out the need for relationship and therefore the need for God. It also destroyed intimacy and the safe environment in which all things could be taught.

A knowledge of God or the world without relationship is just religion. It's information without experience.

Victorious Jesus

Jesus, the last Adam, was victorious in the area that the first Adam was defeated. Temptation was real to both, but Jesus showed us that we could overcome. Just as the first Adam and Jesus, the last Adam, faced temptation, so will we face many temptations. We will have many choices to activate our will or walk in the will of God. Temptation is real and destructive and this is why Jesus calls us to prayer. He knows we need supernatural help to overcome. Temptation is not something we should face alone. The enemy loves to isolate us because he can then manipulate us to do what he wants. We are to overcome every temptation with the deliverer by our side.

Jesus is our model for victory. He showed us how to overcome the devil. With the Word in His mouth, He destroyed every lie and deception the enemy tried to bring. After forty days of prayer and fasting and contending, Jesus faced the enemy and won. He was victorious. He entered the wilderness filled with the Holy Spirit and He returned from the wilderness in the power of the spirit. With every victory, we also move from being filled with to actually experiencing the power of the Holy Spirit.

The garden of Gethsemane

It was in a garden that Adam and Eve had been overcome by temptation and just before the crucifixion, we find Jesus in a garden. The battle is real as He faces the torment of the journey before Him with His ultimate sacrifice on the cross. His sweat turned to blood as He agonized over what was to come. It would have been simple to take an easier route. If only this cup could pass from Him, but it could not. With the disciples praying... well, kind of praying in between sleeping, Jesus prayed.

If not in the exact words but in action, Jesus prayed and demonstrated the very prayer He gave to the disciples. The tools He gave to them, He used Himself. "Lead us not into temptation, but deliver us from the evil one, for Yours is the power and the glory forever. Amen." In His prayer, Jesus subjected His will to the Father's will.

In the Garden of Eden, Adam and Eve chose a tree that looked good. In their temptation, it seemed to offer a more fulfilling life. It was disguised as one thing but gave another. The tree they chose looked beautiful but brought death.

In the Garden of Gethsemane, Jesus prayed among the olive trees. Yet, the only tree that was available to Him looked like death. It would be the place of ultimate surrender and obedience. He laid down His will for the will of the Father. The tree He chose was not as appealing or attractive as the trees around Him, but the tree He chose became the tree of life.

In a Garden, Adam and Eve were tempted and defeated. In a garden, Jesus overcame every temptation to fulfill His destiny. Before us there are many gardens filled with many beautiful things. They are on display and they call our name. Even though they look beautiful and seem to offer much, be careful. Do not make choices according to what you see with your eyes, but what you know is right in your heart. I will go further to say that you should not make decisions independently, but make them in relationship with the Father and you will always make the right decision.

Just as Jesus overcame the devil, so can we overcome the devil. We do not have to face the battle alone. Jesus is now seated at the right hand of the Father as our royal high priest praying and interceding for us.

For we do not have a High Priest who cannot sympathize with our weaknesses, but was in all points tempted as we are, yet without sin.

Let us therefore come boldly before the throne of grace, that we may obtain mercy and find grace to help in our time of need. (Hebrews 4:15-16)

Not only does Jesus know what we are facing and the real power of temptation, He is inviting us to come before the throne of God. Not as one who is overcome with fear, but boldly. We are to come seeking His grace as an overcomer. Let's seek the mercy of God and experience the power of grace that enables us to be victorious. This is a grace that empowers us to overcome in times of need. Grace steps into the place of weakness and gives us strength to do what we struggle to do in the flesh.

I believe that there are areas where you have failed in the past or made the wrong choices that can be changed today. Even as you read this, you can ask for grace. This is not just the grace that covers the sins of the past, though that is the starting point. As long as you feel like you are a failure, you will fail again as it's easy to lose the will to fight. Well, today your past is gone. This is a new day. His mercies are new every morning. With a clean slate, God now wants to give you grace not just to cover your past, but to empower you to live differently today.

Lead Us Not into Temptation

Let us consider the rest of this text in the Lord's Prayer through the eyes of Jesus the victorious one.

Our English translation of "lead us not into temptation" is a little misleading. It may suggest that there are times that God would lead us into temptation. This is never the case. James the half-brother of Jesus said:

> Let no one say when he is tempted, "I am tempted by God"; for God cannot be tempted by evil, nor does he Himself tempt anyone. (James 1:13)

The same James also makes this statement which can cause us to be confused if we do not have proper understanding.

> My brethren, count it all joy when you face various trials. Knowing that the testing of your faith produces patience. But let patience have its perfect work; that you may be perfect and complete lacking nothing. (James 1:2-4)

These two scriptures seem to be talking about the same thing, yet they are very different. Temptation and trials are two different things. They have a different source and a different purpose. One is for good the other is with evil intent.

The problem is the use of the Greek word in this sentence, "lead us not into temptation," and our English interpretation. The Greek word for temptation is "peirasnas" and its meaning can be translated as "temptation, trial or testing". The same Greek word is used for both temptation and trial. However, the context in which the Greek word is used changes its meaning.

When this word is used in a negative way, it is translated as "temptation." The force or personality behind the temptation is the devil. His purpose is to kill, steal, and destroy. It is fueled by the natural man's desire to sin. If we surrender to this temptation, we will be enticed by sin and it will cause us to fall or fail in some way.

When the same Greek word is used in a positive way, it is translated as "trial or testing". Its purpose is to develop you. Through the trial, you will gain something that you didn't have before. You will come out the other side better than you were before the trial. The joy that James speaks of is that which comes as a result of going through the trial. There is a promotion in the making. The battle is not to destroy you, but to establish you.

Another way of looking at this is to say that God has placed an anointing on your life. The anointing is the supernatural ability to do something beyond your natural ability or means. He has given you gifts so He can use you. He has called you to do something special with the gifts He has given you.

Now that you know your gift, God will allow you or place you in a situation to use that gift. He has to activate it and it's best activated in real situations. The test or trial will seem too much for you or beyond your ability to succeed, which it is. This is when the anointing kicks in and enables you or graces you with power to do what you could not do without the anointing. The Holy Spirit will lead you and guide you through this trial. He will speak to you and give you strategies and wisdom that you never thought of before. He will enable you to rise up and use your gift. This process establishes you in the purposes of God.

As you rely on God and use your gift in the midst of the trial, you will go on an adventure of discovery. You will discover something new about God and something new about yourself. You will be forced to use the gifts that have laid dormant in your life. The trial activates the gift. Once you use the gift, you are promoted through the Holy Spirit to a new level of activity. Now you are more equipped for the bigger things that God has promised you.

When we read "lead us not into temptation," it has nothing to do with trials and tests that promote us. There is never a thought that God would lead us into temptation. This prayer, "lead us not into temptation," invites God to keep us, protect us, help us, and deliver us from the temptations we are going through.

It gets better. This temptation was not from God. It is not a test or trial in a positive sense, but there is still a battle to win. It is in these situations that God turns all things for good. That which the devil meant for harm and destruction, God will turn into victory and life.

In the face of trials, the Holy Spirit quickens the gifts and callings of God in our lives. In the face of temptation, the Holy Spirit reveals and illuminates the fruit of the spirit. Tests place our gifts under trial and temptation places our character under attack. The Holy Spirit call us to take up arms and fight for truth and righteousness. The heartbeat of God is to be "holy for I am holy." We are to seek first the kingdom of God and His righteousness.

Even though the enemy wants to destroy us through temptation and sin, God is calling us to righteousness. Every time we stand and overcome temptation, we have another victory. With every victory, the character of God is established in our lives.

God wants us to have victory in every part of our lives. He loves to exult us and place our gifts on display, but He also wants us to reflect His holy character. Just before Jesus went to the cross, we find Him praying for His disciples. We can also see this as a prayer for all who come to Christ.

> I do not pray that You should take them out of the world, but that You should keep them from the evil one. (John 17:15)

This prayer of Jesus recognizes our vulnerability in the world we live. We cannot live this Christian life on our own. Without God, we are not only open to attack, but we are weak at best. Yet, no matter what we face, what dangers we find ourselves in or temptation we are vulnerable to, we can pray. In the moment we face temptation, we don't have to face it alone. God the Father, our great deliverer, is with us and He will keep us. He will protect us and lead us away from the temptations we face.

Like every aspect of the Christian life, we are not walking alone. We are walking hand in hand with the Father. The Lord's Prayer not only emphasizes this, but causes us to acknowledge Him in the face of temptation. You are not on your own. No matter how enticing the temptation may feel or how appealing it is, there is a way out or through this temptation. You are being called to have victory over the enemy.

Our Nature and the Evil One

Temptation comes from two distinct places. Not all temptation is from the devil, even though the devil is the original source of temptation.

Because of the fallen world we live in, we are born with a fallen nature. There is a part of us that loves to sin and walk in unrighteous ways. The temptations we face are part of our old nature or the old man. The new man in Christ chooses to walk differently. Walking and living a righteous lifestyle starts with an upgrade in our thinking. Our mind has to be transformed so we can think like God. Once we see the world like God sees the world, our actions are changed. Proverbs sums this up perfectly by stating, "As a man thinks so am I." If we think like God, we will be more like God in our decision making. If we continue to think like the world, we will fall when trying to resist the various temptations. Our relationships will determine which voice is the most clearly heard in our hearts. Will it be the voice of God or the voice of the world?

Temptation can be a work of the flesh or what our old carnal man wants to do. In fact, the devil might not have much to do with it at all. It's just what we want to do or have. The devil's suggestions or our old nature may just be as simple as reminding us of something we used to enjoy. Sometimes that feeling or urge is enough in itself to lead us astray.

There are other areas of temptation that are a direct result of a full-on, unrelenting assault of the evil one. He is out to destroy us.

When I pray the Lord's Prayer, it brings to my attention both of these areas. "Lead us not into temptation" highlights to me the desires of the flesh. "But deliver us from the evil one" is a revelation of the one behind our thinking and the temptations. What I am saying is that some temptations are to do with our carnal thinking while other temptations are a direct demonic assault upon our hearts and minds.

When it's the work of the flesh, I am praying that God will lead me out of it. I want him to show me another way or door that I can walk through to avoid this pitfall. As we know, there are many pitfalls in the Christian life that will lead to a personal downfall. I am grateful in those moments of weakness that we also know the redeemer and restorer of our soul.

Just because you are a "good" Christian or anointed believer doesn't mean that you will avoid these pitfalls or not fall into sin. When the apostle Paul wrote to the Corinthian church, he recognized them as a church full of gifts. They were "Enriched in everything, in all utterance and knowledge. They did not fall short in any gifting." (1

Corinthians 1:57) Yet, in all these things, they were very immature and carnal in their thinking. It would not take you long to read the books of Corinthians and discover their many errors and failings.

So how do we deal with the old man, the carnal mind, and the works of the flesh? How do we get away from the crazy thoughts that are calling us to do the things we know we shouldn't do? They seem like fun; they are fun. Maybe they give us a buzz, a high, or satisfaction for a moment and then we are left with guilt, or worse, a path of destructive behavior.

By praying "lead us not into temptation" we are inviting God to help us say "no." We are looking to be led away from the things our flesh desires. We are recognizing that we cannot overcome this on our own. Our prayer or request is actually to show me another way to live. The apostle Paul sums up this struggle and answers our cry in the book of Galatians.

> I say then: Walk in the Spirit, and you shall not fulfill the lust of the flesh. For the flesh lusts against the Spirit and the Spirit against the flesh; and these are contrary to one another, so that you do not do the things that you wish. But if you are led by the Spirit you are not under the law. (Galatians 5:16-18)

We know that our flesh man and spirit man want two different things. The struggle is real between the things that this world offers and the things of the kingdom of God. The apostle Paul points out a way of victory. It's the same way that Jesus overcame in His wilderness experience and temptation. Jesus was led by the Spirit. (Matthew 4:1) We, also, should be led by the Holy Spirit. Let's choose to yield to His leading and not to that of our flesh.

When we pray "lead us not into temptation," we are inviting the Holy Spirit to lead us in another direction. We are asking for His strength to help us overcome. We are seeking His wisdom to do the right thing and not the wrong thing. We are looking for His grace to be poured out upon us before we sin. It is a grace that gives us power and authority to overcome at the place of temptation. If we receive the grace and power of God at the beginning stages of temptation, we will not need the grace and covering mercy of God after we sin.

When we are led by the Holy Spirit, He often leads with a positive outlook and not a negative outlook. He places within us a bigger "yes" than a big "no." What do I mean by that? Our human nature is often left intrigued by the words "no, you can't have this or don't do that." The rebellious heart shouts out against what others say we can and can't do and we often want to just try it, just once, so we know what it feels like.

The bigger "yes" of the Holy Spirit is the brighter outlook. It's the reason why we say "no" to temptation. It's the victory it brings and the hope for a better future.

The Evil One

Jesus is very clear regarding where the second area of temptation comes from. It's not just a feeling, urge, or desire that's come out of our fallen human nature. It a demonic attack; the work of the evil one.

We have to discern and understand where the battle is being waged. If it is in our flesh, then we need to invite the Holy Spirit to lead us into victory. If the attack is from the evil one, we need to take a stand and fight. In this battle against the devil, we still need to ask the Holy Spirit to lead us. He has a battle strategy that will enable us to overcome.

That battle strategy may be to lift up the double edged sword, the Word of God, and speak truth. It is through the Word of God that we overcome the lies and manipulation of the evil one. It may be that we wage warfare with the prophetic words we have received in the past with a promise of a better future.

We can also change the environment by entering a time of praise and worship. This creates a place in which we invite God to inhabit our praise; a place the enemy cannot stay. It also changes our thought process from what the devil wants us to do to who God is. We start to gaze on the nature of the Father and all the promises He has for us. We reset our focus and thinking. Through praise, we pull down all the imaginations and illusions of the enemy. We replace the temptations that have been exalted in our thinking by exalting Christ in our praise. This brings all exalted thoughts, imaginations and lies under the subjection of the knowledge of Christ. (2 Corinthians 10:5)

Like any battle, we may not be able to overcome on our own. We may need other believers to come alongside us. This is always scary because we fear that if we confess the temptations we have, we will be judged. We think we will be made to feel unworthy even though we have not necessarily sinned. This is a great plot of the enemy. He knows that the moment you share with others, you will be strengthened by them to overcome.

There is Another Door

No matter how severe the attack, God will always give you the ability to overcome. He will either give you a strategy in which you are able to bear the temptation or He will provide a way of escape.

No temptation has overtaken you except such as is common to man; but God is faithful, who will not allow you to be tempted beyond what you are able, but with the temptation will also make the way of escape, that you may be able to bear it. (1 Corinthians 10:13)

There is always a door or a way out. For some, the door is very obvious. We see this in the life of Joseph. Many of you know the story of Joseph. He was seen as his father's favorite and he wore a precious coat of many colors. He was a son who had a great dream. In his dream, his father, mother, and brothers came to serve him. His dream was from God and eventually came true. One day his brother would be grateful for the dream and the deliverance that he brought, but in the moment, they were not happy. They did not like the thought of serving their younger brother and they did not like the dreams he had.

This dream caused the brothers to become angry and they wanted to kill Joseph. They threw him into a pit and wanted him to die. They did not need his dreams. When they couldn't follow through with their murderous intentions, they sold him into slavery. Joseph ended up in the house of Potiphar, an Egyptian captain.

The hand and favor of God was on Joseph and so he grew in influence in Potiphar's house. Joseph prospered in all he did and he was entrusted as overseer in his master's house and over all that he owned.

The anointing and gifts of God cause us to be exalted. They mark a person as different. People see what God is doing and they like it; they are attracted to the anointing. Some are attracted to what God is doing and have good intentions, while others have evil intentions.

Potiphar was pleased with Joseph's servant's heart and he promoted him. Potiphar's wife was attracted to what she saw, but she wanted Joseph for herself. She made no secret of her desire and asked Joseph to lay with her.

This is a real life temptation. He had all that his master's house offered and now the final jewel in the crown was being offered to him. He, the servant, could take all that the master had. Joseph refused to give in to this temptation. He saw the door, an obvious door, and made a run for it.

For Joseph, the door before him was plain to see. He had to get away from the very thing that was a temptation. For us, the door is often that clear and we have to run. This is one of the only areas where running from an enemy is actually victory over the enemy.

At other times, the door or way of escape may not be so obvious. It may even present itself a long time before we are in the heavy battle of temptation. In fact, if we take the door that God gives us, we may not have to go through some temptations at all.

King David is one of my favorite characters in the Bible. He is a mighty warrior, a great leader, and a king that has a heart after God's own heart. As we read the Old Testament, we travel with David from being a boy to a man. We follow from his anointing and the promise that he will be king, to seeing him ruling and reigning as the king. We see victory after victory. We sing the very songs and Psalms he wrote in both the valley and on the mountain top.

Suddenly, we are somewhat stunned into silence. The giant killer, our great king, is overcome by his desire for a beautiful young woman. She catches his gaze as she baths on the rooftop. He has seen her and can't get the thought of her out of his head. He wants what he knows is not his to take. She belonged to another man. Pride rises up. He is the king and he can have what he wants. We know the rest of the story and the king's failure. Lives are broken, families destroyed, and her husband ends up dead. Only God can redeem the mess and in God's great grace, He does.

This is not a time to start shaking the finger of self-righteousness. We should always seek to do what the apostle Paul tells us to do. We should seek to restore such who have fallen in a spirit of gentleness, lest we also fall into temptation.

What we can do is ask a question with the intention of avoiding the same pitfalls. My question would be, "How could he have avoided this error or sin?" If we can find the solution, we may be saved from the same failure. After all, God promised a way or door of escape. So where was the way of escape? The Bible tell us:

> _It happened in the spring of the year, at the time when kings go out to battle, that David sent besieged Rabboah, But David remained at Jerusalem._
>
> _Then it happened one evening that David arose from his bed and walked on the roof the king's house. And from the roof he saw a women bathing, and the women was very beautiful to behold. (2 Samuel 11:1-2)_

The door of escape came before the temptation started. "It happened" signifies that this was a key event. David's door of escape was to do what he had been called and anointed to do. He was the king and as the king, he was to lead the men in battle. Up until this point, David had been the perfect leader. He was strong and at the forefront of the battle. On this occasion, he decided to stay home. We have no idea why he decided to stay home, but he did. It was the wrong decision.

When we are not doing what we should be doing or when we don't go through the doors that God opens, other doors open up to us. We are left vulnerable and in the midst of another kind of battle; a battle for righteousness. In a place of idleness in the middle of the night, we become most vulnerable. What should have been another great victory in battle turns into a dark season of the soul in the heart of David.

God always give us a door of escape. This door may be like the one that Joseph saw. It is obvious and we have to make a run for it. However, in many cases, the door is a door of kingdom activity. It is what we should be doing. It's a place of calling and service.

The battle over temptation is sometimes won by taking a defensive approach. We quench all of the fiery darts of the enemy with the shield of faith. We run for the cover of escape that God has provided and we win. However, more often than not, we are to be offensive in battle. We take up the weapons of warfare which are the gifts and calling of God. We walk through the doors of kingdom activity and by doing so, we are not left open to the attacks of the enemy and the temptations he brings.

Discerning of Spirits

We can put this another way. When I pray the Lord's Prayer and ask God not to lead me into temptation, I am asking Him to lead me into victory. What I am really asking for is the gift of discernment. Give me eyes to clearly see what is going on. Place me as a watchman of the Lord who can see both the enemy approaching and the victory before me.

For me, the gift of discernment is not just asking God what the devil is doing. It's also asking God what He is doing. It's choosing the door long before temptation is an issue. Discernment is not just revealing the kingdom of darkness, but also the kingdom of light. The gift of discernment will not only lead me away from trouble, but more often, it will lead me into kingdom activity that keeps me from trouble or the temptations of the enemy.

When we read about the gifts of the Holy Spirit in 1 Corinthians 12, the apostle Paul warns us not to be ignorant. We should have understanding of the gifts. I think that most people who move in the gifts of the Holy Spirit have a good understanding about what they are and what they do. That is with the exception of the gift of discernment. I think most in the church think they know what it is, but they see it in a one dimensional way. Many think this gift is given just so we can discern what the devil is up to. This is a truth, but only a partial truth. I think we have become lazy or ignorant in our understanding due to what we have been taught.

The gift of discernment is actually called the gift of "discerning of spirits." (1 Corinthians 12.11) Spirits is not singular as in one area of discernment but plural, meaning more than one area of spirits to discern. When we read the Bible, we can actually see four different spirits in operation. I want to just take a little time to explain this as I believe it's important to understand discernment in line with the way we pray.

The first spirit is the Holy Spirit. He was given to us by the Father when Jesus rose again. The Holy Spirit lives in us and never leaves us. At the same time, He comes upon us in power so we can move in power. He is like no other. He is a pure genius, full of wisdom and is a perfect reflection of the Father and Son. He is the one who leads us in the will of God. He guides us into God's goodness. He releases the gifts of the spirit through us and produces the fruit of the spirit in us.

Next, there are angelic beings, which are also called spirits. We are told in the book of Hebrews that the angels are ministering spirits known as flames of fire. They have been sent to minister to those who inherit salvation through Christ Jesus. (Hebrews 1:7 & 14) We see that Jesus was ministered to by angels after His wilderness experience. (Matthew 4:11) If there was a time that Jesus could be ministered to by angels, then we can also expect times when we may also be ministered to by angels.

The third area is the human spirit. That which is in you. The human spirit can be easily influenced by good or bad. The human spirit is subject to environments, the supernatural, words we speak, the things we read, or anything we give and surrender our lives to.

Our spirit can and is influenced by God. We are told that the Holy Spirit strengthens our human spirit or our inner man. (Ephesians 4:16) The Holy Spirit bears witness with our human spirit, confirming that we are children of God. (Romans 8:16)

Just as the Holy Spirit can influence the spirit of man, so can other things influence our spirit. We can have a broken spirit or wounded spirit. (Proverbs 17:22 & Proverbs 18:14) Our spirit can be crushed or even oppressed by the devil.

The truth is that we need to discern the spirit at work, but in the case of the human spirit, it can be good or bad. When influenced by the Holy Spirit, we can be used to bring the kingdom in a more pure way. But when we minister or live from a wounded or oppressed spirit, we will minister truth funneled through our bad experiences. That which comes through us is no longer pure truth but tainted truth and therefore a mistruth.

The fourth area of spirits is evil spirits. This is the devil, the evil one, demons, principalities and powers, strongholds, spirits of darkness and thrones of wickedness. (Ephesians 6:12) These spirits are at war against us. The good news is that we are on the winning side. We have been made complete in Christ Jesus who is the head over principalities and powers. (Colossians 2:10)

As we come to understand these four areas, we realize that the discerning of spirits is understanding which of these four areas is at work.

This area of discernment is seen in the ministry of Paul the apostle. We read that there was a time in which he tried to go into Asia. It was the next place on his list to visit. As he went from city to city, he tried to enter Asia. The Holy Spirit told him not to go. (Acts 16:6)

Paul continued to try to go into other areas but the Holy Spirit would not let him. Then, during the night, Paul had a dream. In the dream, a man from Macedonia appeared to him. He pleaded with Paul to come and preach the gospel. When Paul awoke, he knew or discerned that this was the Holy Spirit leading him.

Paul followed the leading of the Spirit and went to Macedonia. The outcome was that they had a divine encounter, meaning a meeting set up by God, with a woman called Lydia. This woman surrendered her life to Christ and a church was started in her home. The gift of discernment in this case lead Paul into the will of God.

Just after this experience, we read about another story that needs discernment. Paul is on his way to pray and a girl starts to follow him. As she follows him, she starts to cry out that they are men of God. The things she was saying seemed to be right, but something felt wrong. Something was wrong.

This girl had a demonic spirit in her life; a spirit of divination. In the beginning, Paul had no idea what was going on but he was greatly annoyed by her actions and words. She followed Paul and those with him for days. Then suddenly, Paul realized what was happening. He realized that this girl was being used by an evil spirit. With great boldness he rebuked the evil spirit and it came out of her. (Acts 16:16-18)

Paul used the same gift of "discerning of spirits" for two totally different areas. Discernment was used to understand both the will of God and the plots of the enemy.

Discernment and the Lord's Prayer

I love to pray this part of the Lord Prayer because what I am really asking for is discernment. By praying "lead me not into temptation," I am also praying for God to show me what I should be doing. I want to see the doors that God has opened to me long before temptations comes. I want to go to war in the times that kings go to war.

At the same time, I am also asking that God would deliver me from the evil one. I want to see what the enemy is doing. I need discernment to know what is the desire of my flesh or human spirit or what is a demonic spirit. Once we know the source, we know how to stand. If it's the human spirit, we can surrender to the Holy Spirit who will lead us into all truth. If it's a demonic spirit, we can fight a spiritual warfare and overcome.

Our Great Deliverer

Finally, I want to emphasis the role of the great deliverer. There are many ways in which the evil one will try to lead us into sin. Whatever the battle, the strategy of God gives us the ability to overcome. God is with us. The moment we pray, "lead us not into temptation but deliver us," we are inviting the great "deliverer" to intervene and help us.

God is our great deliverer. He will never leave us alone to fight a battle. He will always be the light in darkness, the still voice in the noise of battle. He is a safe place, the rock upon which we stand. He is our fortress and our deliverer.

When most people read this part of the Lord's Prayer, the first words they see are "temptation" and "evil one." That may be because they are approaching God out of a place of fear. They might find themselves in circumstances that are difficult. They may be facing some of their own demons. These temptation and desires are calling them to do something they know they should not be doing. They are transfixed on the problem and fail to see the solution.

The first thing I see when I read or pray this are the words "deliver us." I know our God will step in and rescue me or make a way out. This is backed up by the words, "For Yours is the Kingdom and the power and the glory, forever. Amen."

This final sentence not only underlines the power of the Lord's Prayer in general, but it emphasizes the power of the deliverer in the midst of the temptation of the evil one. In the kingdom of God, there are no equal forces. The darkness or the devil is not an equal opposing power to God who is the light. The devil cannot live in the same glory of God. In fact, he was cast out of His glory or the presence of God. There is only one winner in the kingdom and that is God. He rules supreme. He lives in you and at every opportunity or invitation you give Him, He works through you. That places you on the winning side.

As we pray this, God the deliverer is standing at your side. He is calling on the warrior within you. He wants you to stand and continue to stand against every lie and temptation of the devil. He is raising a champion and even though you may have fallen in the past, He is calling you to rise and fight another day. He is making you into an overcomer. That which overcame you yesterday is subject to you today. Not only are His mercies new every morning, but we can pray the Lord's Prayer every day and experience the power of the deliverer.

Final Thoughts

Our Father and His Great Names

My desire is that through this little book you not only find greater understanding in the Lord's Prayer, but a lifestyle of prayer. A prayer that shapes your relationship with the Father and repositions you as sons and daughters. In the words of a popular song, you are no longer slaves! This is a time in your life to not only worship (hallowed be) His name, but live under all that His name declares that He is for you and in you.

Your Kingdom Come

Let this be a time when you surrender your castle for His kingdom. Let heaven invade earth with all its power and glory. Cultivate a place in which you live out of a supernatural expectation. Transforming the very things that seem impossible into possibilities.

Your will be done

The days of your prayers not being answered are over for your prayers are no longer yours, they are a reflection of His heart and will. You are no longer just praying to God but with God. You have been given a promise and a confidence that He will give you the partitions you have asked of Him because they are in partnership with His desires.

Daily Bread

This day you no longer live void of God but filled with God. You can come boldly before the throne of grace and ask for bread; the bread of life that is both Jesus the person and the provider. It is the bread that He provides for your daily need and the spiritual bread that proceeds out of the mouth of God and sustains your spirit man.

Forgiveness

The way has been made open for you to come and ask for forgiveness and enjoy the journey of redemption. This is the place in His presence in which you are washed and transformed by His love. Your prayer to Him becomes a prayer with Him as you partner together and cry out for your enemies.

Deliver Us

Today you realize His supreme power and glory. You have not been left to fight alone against temptation or the evil one. The great deliverer is on your side.

Today is a day of victory and a day of power. It is a day in which you don't just cry out to God in hope of being rescued or heard. Through relationship, you have been embraced by the Father. You, in turn, have been embraced by your Papa and together the kingdom of God is released from heaven to earth.

Other Books by Pastor Darren Farmer:

Broken: Restoration For God's Wounded

Jesus came for the lost, the hurting, the sinner, and those who have been rejected by man. So why is it that the church is full of wounded people who feel that they have failed God or messed up so badly that there is no return? *Broken* is an inspirational book about how God wants to reach out with arms of grace to the wounded, calling the prodigals home. Jesus not only welcomes all people, He desires to bring full restoration to those who have fallen into sin.

This book will not only help individuals who have gone through various kinds of failure, it will also offer guidance for pastors, church leaders, and counsellors as they help those who have failed in some area of their life. This book inspires people to come into a place of hope, enabling them to re-engage in the church and dream again.

Awakening the Issachar Generation

Nothing is as it seems – everything is how God sees it!

When we look at the world in which we live and consider the seasons of life we journey through, without a kingdom perspective, we are left with a false picture of reality.

In John 4, the disciples knew there were still four months until the harvest. But Jesus instructed them to "lift up their eyes and look at the fields because they were already white for harvest." Jesus spoke of the spiritual climate while the disciples were fixed on the natural.

When we "look up" to see and understand the times we are in, our reality changes.

It is time to look up and see life from God's vantage point and allow Him to transform your seasons.

Just as "....the sons of Issachar who had understanding of the times, to know what Israel ought to do..." (1 Chronicles 12:32)

These books are available through the following:

www.deeperworshipcenter.net

www.amazon.com

amazon worldwide - Select the Amazon website in your nation

www.kindle.amazon.com

Pastor Darren Farmer is an inspirational preacher with a desire to see the supernatural power of God restored in the church. Some have called him a "fire starter" and others have called him a "revivalist." However, Darren's primary goal is to see the body of Christ equipped and mobilized and doing the work of God in our everyday lives. He believes ministry is not contained in the church, but flows into every area of life that we touch.

Pastor Darren graduated from The School of Prophets Bible School in Birmingham, England. He has been involved in full time Apostolic ministry since he started his first church, The Sanctuary, in 1995.

The Sanctuary grew rapidly and Pastor Darren realized the need to expand. A new Bible school was established called "The Apostolic School of Ministry." Through the school, five new churches were established in England and seven new churches in Nigeria.

In 2005, Darren heard the call of God to leave the UK and move to the United States to pastor an established church in Bangor, Maine. Since then, Darren and his wife, Amanda, have established a new church, Deeper Worship Center, in Portland, Maine. They continue to pastor this church and see the presence of God touching lives in new ways every week.

Darren continues to travel and minister with a desire to see hearts set on fire and the kingdom released. God is using him to call the church to go "deeper" in worship, in the Word, and in the works of the Holy Spirit.

For More Information:

You can find Pastor Darren's contact information on the web:

www.deeperworshipcenter.net

Email: pastordarrendwc@gmail.com

Please contact us if you would like to invite Pastor Darren and Amanda Farmer to minister at your church.

We would love to hear your testimony as result of reading this book.

Made in the USA
Middletown, DE
09 April 2019